Loch Ness Monster

By the same author

The Leviathans

Project Water Horse

LOCH NESS MONSTER

Tim Dinsdale AMRAeS

Routledge & Kegan Paul   London, Henley and Boston

First published 1961
Reprinted 1966
Second edition 1972
Third edition 1976
by Routledge & Kegan Paul Ltd
39 Store Street,
London WC1E 7DD,
Broadway House,
Newtown Road,
Henley-on-Thames,
Oxon RG9 1EN and
9 Park Street
Boston, Mass. 02108, USA
Printed in Great Britain by
Unwin Brothers Limited,
Woking and London

ISBN 0 7100 8395 5 (c)
ISBN 0 7100 8394 7 (p)

To those who search the 'Beastie' out

Contents

Illustrations

Preface

During the course of the last fifteen years I have had the privilege of working at Loch Ness on the search and research operations which are today a source of international interest and discussion.

This book is about the Loch Ness Monster or rather the family of huge, as yet unidentified aquatic animals of extraordinary appearance which inhabit this famous—one might almost say infamous—deep, dark body of fresh water in the Scottish Highlands.

It also tells the story of the search for them which involves a great many people and ideas and events and mistakes and successes.

It is a true story.

TD

Acknowledgments

I would like to thank the following for permission to reproduce photographs: the *Daily Mail*, Plate No. 1; Mr H. L. Cockrell, Plate No. 2; Mr P. A. Macnab, Plate No. 3; Stuart Markson, Plate No. 8; Academy of Applied Science and Jet Propulsion Laboratories, Plate No. 9; the British Museum (Natural History), Plate No. 12; Mr. R. H. Lowrie, Plate No. 13.

I am much indebted also to Mrs R. T. Gould for permission to quote from the books *The Case for the Sea Serpent* and *The Loch Ness Monster and Others*, and to Mrs Constance Whyte for permission to quote from her book *More than a Legend* published by Hamish Hamilton.

I am deeply grateful to all the many friends and acquaintances who have contributed to this book, or helped with their advice and encouragement; particularly, Alex Campbell, Hugh and Jane Rowand, Father J. A. Carruth, Bill Hutchison, Dick Clarke and George Pipal, Bruce Ing, Peter Baker, Col. Patrick Grant, Mrs Marjory Moir, Mrs Greta Finlay, Mr Hugh Gray, Mrs Gladys Macdonald, Mrs Marjorie Croil, Mr Michael Peacock, Mr Alan Marshall, Mr Coppin, Mrs Hilda Bromley, Admiral Henderson, Mr A. Cruickshank, Mr Michael Randolph, Mr William Palmer, Mr H. L. Cockrell, Mr P. A. Macnab, Mr John Carr, to Liz and Torquil MacLeod, Jim Ewing, Colin Franklin, the Rev. W. L. Dobb, Miss M. Bridgman, David James, Ken Peterson, Ken Wallis, Holly Arnold, Rip Hepple, Liz Montgomery-Campbell and others of the Loch Morar Survey Team; Bob and Carol Rines, Marty Klein, Ike Blonder, Bob Needleman, Charles Wyckoff, Harold Edgerton, Alan Gillespie, Olaf-Willums of the Academy team; Kenneth Warr and John Sanders of the Royal Photographic Society; Peter Byrne and Celia Kileen of the Big Foot Information Centre; Jim Buchanan of Undersea Vision (Scotland) Ltd; Andy Wheeler, Ivor Newby and Lee Frank who dive courageously; Nick Witchell, Dick and Phyllis Jenkyns, Basil and 'Freddie' Cary and all my friends at 'home port' Fort Augustus.

1 The spark

There can be few people in the English-speaking world today who have never heard of the fabled 'Loch Ness Monster', that curious half mythical creature which is supposed to inhabit the forbidding black depths of water of Scotland's biggest loch; and yet there can be fewer still who know anything about it, or who claim to have actually seen the beast. Until the month of March in 1959, I was not one of these people. I knew nothing about it at all, and probably did not believe in it, though I had never bothered to think about it very much; and then, late one evening, glancing through the pages of a small magazine I particularly liked to read, my eye came to rest on a printed photograph, and next to it a bold heading in capital letters—'The Day I saw the Loch Ness Monster'.

I examined the photograph with mild curiosity, but could make out nothing more than an indeterminate sinuous shape floating on the glassy surface of a lake, and in the background a distant shore and tree-clad hills rising abruptly. Gazing at the article more intently, however, I became aware of a growing interest. Before my eyes ran the serious, carefully chosen words of men and women who claimed to have seen a huge and fantastic beast like some great dinosaur of prehistoric times, churning the waters of Loch Ness to a foam, or swimming off across it at tremendous speed, trailing a wake like that from a speedboat, with waves breaking on the shore half a mile behind.

I read that on one occasion in 1933 a very reputable couple, a company director and his wife, driving down the road close to the lochside in the early-morning light, claimed to have actually seen this creature on land, crossing the road ahead, lurching towards the water in fright, its great barrel-like body preceded by ten feet of snake-like undulating neck—and these were people who professed to have had no knowledge, at the time, that a monster was even supposed to exist!

The article briefly covered the history of events and more impressive sightings, leading up to the present day, describing how the legend had grown through centuries from the ancient time of St Columba, when 'some water monster' was first reported within the borders of the loch; and how the story of the Gaelic 'Eigh-Uisge', or water horse had survived, passed on from father to son, from fisherman to woodsman, prompted and sustained by the rare but apparently real appearance of the beast. Then in 1933, with the construction of a modern motor road close to the loch, along its northern shore from Inverness to Fort Augustus, a sudden spate of reports had come in, following the first published account obtained on May 22 of that year from a Mr John McKay and his wife, when driving one day along this newly completed road.

It appeared obvious this sudden influx of stories and reports owed much to the large-scale felling of trees and shrubs as the construction of the road progressed, exposing to view a great part of the loch which for uncounted centuries had lain silently remote, viewed only by the eyes of local fishermen; but equally perhaps the shattering din of blasting echoing back and forth from crag to crag, and the plunging descent of great quantities of rock to the bottom of the loch hundreds of feet below, frightened these strange creatures, forcing them to the surface with a frequency that has never since been equalled.

Reading on, I learned of the first serious attempt to solve the mystery. In 1934 Sir Edward Mountain had put a private expedition into the field at his own expense. He arranged for twenty men to view the loch from nine in the morning until dusk, with cameras at the ready. The search lasted for thirty days and although a number of still photographs and a few feet of 16 mm. film were exposed on the Monster, the results were inconclusive.

All the pictures had been taken at too great a range and showed little more than the wash the animal made, or a small part of its back, the scale of which was very difficult to judge. From then on, the Monster began to fall into disrepute; inevitably there were jokes and hoaxes—some merely foolish, and others ingenious, fooling the press and public for a while and then dissolving away into laughter, prejudicing thought; turning the Monster into a laughing stock, the butt of every music-hall comedian, —a source of international mirth.

The years began to roll by; and although reports continued to come in from various parts of the loch, no one paid much attention to them, and those who claimed to have seen the beast suffered so much ridicule they wished they had remained anonymous. The war came, putting an end to rumours for a while, but when it was over the legend of the Monster revived, brought back to life by new accounts of sightings and then, in 1957, a book was published. It had been written by a woman, who collected the facts and the photographs and presented them for all to see, constructing a case for the Monster which few people could doubt, and in so doing, planted the seed from which began to sprout, in time, a reawakened interest. . .

Putting the magazine down, I sat in thought for a moment. True, the article appeared to have been written with the professional polish of a journalist, condensing facts and other people's statements, but undoubtedly it had a ring of truth about it. I was mentally disturbed; jolted out of the rut of normal thinking by this detailed and strange account of the Monster—or fish, or reptile, or throw-back from the past or whatever it might be; but more important perhaps, it was immediately clear to me that either a large number of different people were prepared to tell the most fantastic lies in print—and therefore in public; or alternatively the truth, or what they sincerely believed to be the truth.

The possibility they could be mistakenly describing some quite ordinary object floating in the loch seemed hardly probable, in view of the categoric statements made about a long sinuous neck and little head protruding above the surface, attached to a huge and powerful body, with a tail capable of throwing up a wash like that from a small steamer! Surely no one could be that much mistaken, and certainly not a whole collection of different people over a period of thirty years or more, who all said much the same about it. No, there must be a core of truth in the story; explainable perhaps, when one knew the facts, but nevertheless a core of truth.

I read the article through a second time and sat turning it over in my mind, bewildered, and then decided to show it to my wife and see how she reacted to it. I passed the magazine to her, without an explanation, asking for her opinion. She sat down to study it, and as her eyes picked up the thread of text I watched her expression carefully, for this is part of what she read:

The early morning mist was clearing fast as I came out of my cottage on the banks of Loch Ness. It was a June morning in 1934. Then as the mist shredded away under the warm sunlight, I witnessed the most incredible sight I have seen in my forty years as a water bailiff on Scotland's biggest Loch. Something rose from the water like a monster of pre-historic times, measuring a full thirty feet from tip to tail. It had a long sinuous neck and a flat reptilian head. Its skin was greyish black, tough looking, and just behind, where the neck joined the body, was a giant hump like that on a camel, though many times bigger. I pinched myself hard, but it was no dream, the Loch Ness Monster out there in the water was real and tangible. For several minutes it lay there contentedly, basking in the early sunlight.

The sound of a couple of herring drifters approaching from the lower basin of the Caledonian canal broke the spell, and as the drifters came nearer, it lowered its long neck and dived under the dark surface of the loch, disappearing in a turmoil of water and sending up a miniature tidal wave.

I have seen one of these strange denizens of the Loch (for there are certainly more than one) several times since. But never quite so clearly . . .*

My wife said: 'I think there's probably something in it—these tales of a Monster have been going on for years and years, so there *must* be something unusual in the loch, or there wouldn't be so much fuss about it!'

We both agreed the stories must stem either from a lot of journalistic bunkum or alternatively from a foundation of truth; but the first possibility, the one to which one would most naturally turn perhaps considering what was said, did not, in fact, hold water under close examination. In the early thirties, the story of the Monster claimed world-wide notoriety, affecting not just one or two newspapers, but hundreds, and although the press might be expected to welcome and assist the development of a tale such as this, it would hardly have invented it. The press might at first have been taken in by some of the more famous hoaxes—but again, most of these had been exposed as hoaxes, leaving behind a mass of consistently similar reports for which there remained no logical explanation at all; reports in which people were quite definite and explicit about the huge size and extra-ordinary appearance of the object, and its ability to create a disturbance in the loch on a scale beyond the scope of the most ingenious hoaxer.

It was disturbing—there was something strange about it, something quite unexplained, and yet something quite convincing. I kept turning the story over in my mind, and, late that night in bed, fitfully asleep, I dreamt I walked the steep jutting shores of the loch, and peered down at the inky waters—searching for the Monster; waiting for it to burst from the depths just as I had read, and as the wan light of dawn filtered

* *Everybody's* Magazine, 21 February 1959, Mr Alex Campbell's account.

through the curtains, I awoke and knew the imaginary search beginning so clearly in my dream had grown into fact, and that as time wore on I must bend both purpose and my will to the study of this very strange phenomenon. I knew I had fallen victim once more to a recurrent virus from which I had suffered on and off for years—the germ of curiosity; and recognizing the symptoms I knew there was no escape.

Later that day I found time to mull the facts over once more and decide a course of action. I had already been through the article several times and although I felt an urge to jump in the car and rush off to the loch, common sense forbade such impulsive action; and so did the prospect of paying for the journey, a round trip of a thousand miles or so! I decided to analyse the story, with a view perhaps to finding further hidden clues as to details of appearance, habit, or behaviour—anything in fact that might lead to a better understanding, or suggest an effective line of action. With concentration, I studied the article paragraph by paragraph, making notes about it, and at the end of half an hour summed up. There were five points worth consideration.

Firstly: of the ten or so sightings recorded, the majority seemed to have occurred in the very early morning, just after dawn, and this suggested the animal might conform to a routine or be nocturnal in habit; this could also explain why it was so rarely seen, although on the basis of a few reports it would be a mistake to draw any firm conclusions.

Secondly: people, completely disassociated and reliable people, seemed to say much the same about it and indicated surprise and astonishment in terms that were both simple and candid; and this suggested truth.

Thirdly: that in spite of the promise of Sir Edward Mountain's expedition in 1934, no official expedition had ever visited the loch, in all the years that followed, in spite of the continued flow of evidence.

Fourthly: hoaxes, confusing though they may have been, had generally been exposed as such, and did not appear to explain the hard core of evidence.

Fifthly: due to the relatively narrow width of the loch averaging a mile and a quarter right down its 24-mile length, the surface could be put within range and scan of a number of telephoto cameras, mounted at points of vantage on either side—and in appreciation of this last very important fact, I decided to take action.

What had gone on before at the loch was really of little importance in the sense that the Monster was now officially 'dead' anyway, and if opportunities had been missed, and information misinterpreted in days gone by, the only remedy lay in obtaining fresh evidence of a kind that was both believable and acceptable to science, and that would mean film, clear ciné film, recording without fear of doubt the existence of the animal—if in fact it did exist, and was not the product of Highland whisky after all.

The prospect of constructing a master plan for a campaign of observation posed a number of interesting problems, and at the first opportunity I set to work, attempting to eliminate the more obvious of these in logical sequence, and before long possessed the bones of a workable scheme, of over-ambitious proportions. In the weeks that followed I made attempts to gain support for it, but without success—it proved a dismal failure. No one, it seemed, had time or money to spare for crack-pot expeditions, and I came to realize that without more convincing evidence there could be little hope of success, and yet without financial help and the co-operative efforts of many people, the chance of getting this evidence was very slim indeed. Sir Edward Mountain's expedition had shown that if one individual watched the loch for thirty days, during the hours of daylight, he might, with luck, see the Monster on *one* occasion.

I decided to remodel the plan on less extravagant lines and try again—but before it was complete I had read the book about the Monster: *More than a Legend*, by Constance Whyte. Here were the facts I so badly needed, collected and arranged by an educated person, wife of the Caledonian Ship Canal manager at Loch Ness; experienced in twenty-three years of first-hand Monster lore. I read through her book quickly, intrigued by what I saw: photographs, sketches, maps and statements, accurate testimony to this modern fairy tale, and, as I read these chapters I came to realize there was much to learn, and that it would indeed be foolish to present a plan to any authority in the hope of winning support until I knew a great deal more of this very complex subject. It would first be wise to study the evidence in greater detail, and try to become an expert on the subject.

I set to work, committing several hours each evening to the intimate study of facts, so clearly stated by Mrs Whyte. I read through the book again, comparing what was said by different people, and in this, a large scale map proved useful, allowing me to form a picture of the place of which she wrote; and a strange place it appeared to be, with towering cliffs, rivers and shingle beaches dotting the perimeter of a great sheet of water, plunging down to an awesome depth directly off the shore—six and seven hundred feet deep in places. But, the more I examined the facts about the Monster, the more puzzled I became. How could such a creature exist—in overcrowded Britain, bursting with people and motor cars? It was simply beyond comprehension, and yet in the words of ordinary folk I was sure I had read the truth; but again, how could it be that in spite of all the evidence, there had never been a full-scale scientific expedition?

This aspect of the problem was the most difficult to understand: but there had to be an explanation for it. I remembered the foolish hoaxes in the early thirties. At this time, Science had begun to take an interest in the Monster, but, one day, the footprints of some strange animal had appeared in the mud on the shores of the loch, and were reported by a man who claimed to speak as an expert on the spoor of larger animals. He said the marks differed from any he had seen in a lifetime of big-game hunting. In due course plaster casts were taken and sent to the British Museum—only to prove the fake, for fake it certainly was; the prints had been formed by the foot of a female hippopotamus, the dried remains of some hunter's trophy. A hoax like this could prove both a humorous and misleading thing, accentuated in the public eye because it at first succeeded, frightening off the men of science, just as they were about to act; and following on the Monster had become a laughing stock. Professional men with reputations at stake no longer dared to talk about it, and perhaps welcomed an excuse to drop the subject, and so, the years had rolled by. The war passed, and as time went on it added strength to the now certain belief the Monster was a fake, a figment of the times and popular imagination, adding to the ever tightening vicious circle of doubt and inactivity.

I stopped to consider these facts again, for here perhaps lay the answer to the most curious part of the riddle—the extraordinary lack of scientific interest.

Point number one: The verbal evidence that existed was unacceptable to science, and yet nothing effective had ever been done to obtain evidence that *was* acceptable.

Point number two: The passage of time had destroyed both incentive to act and belief in what was said about the Monster, and the more that passed reduced the chances that anything would ever be done about it.

I realized the significance of this simple theory. If it was in fact correct, and witnesses were indeed correct in what they had reported—the most extraordinary zoological discovery of the century might yet be confirmed within the shores of Loch Ness by any man willing to test his luck and initiative!

I decided to continue to study the cases both for and against the Monster, but at the same time prepare a plan of reconnaissance, to be put into effect as soon as I could arrange it. Only by so doing would it be possible to test this theory against the back-drop of reality posed by the great loch itself; and if I could not persuade others to join me in the hunt, I would have to search the loch unaided, and hope that good fortune and perhaps the right technique and equipment would combine to lessen the almost hopeless odds. It was November: the earliest I could get away would be in the spring of the following year, Easter-time perhaps, when trees were bare, affording an unrestricted view of the loch—but in the months that lay between I would have the time to think about the problem.

2 Jig-saw puzzle

During the winter of 1959 I had the opportunity of studying the Monster seriously, but before attempting to analyse the subject, it was first necessary to decide how best this could be done.

To begin with I faced the inevitable in the form of second-hand evidence, and no matter how much I felt inclined to believe these reports, or the people who recorded them, they remained second-hand, and there appeared to be no ready means of getting first-hand evidence until I went to the loch myself. That did not mean these accounts could not be used, but it did mean that I would have to accept them all in good faith, and treat each with an equal degree of objective detachment; and also that the analysis would (in theory) have to cater for all standards of reports varying from the unembellished truth to downright lies, perhaps, and if it was still to reflect the truth it would have to be based on a great number of reports, far more than necessary had I been able to assess the value of each at first hand.

I decided on a hundred eye-witness reports as a minimum. As all of these were to be treated with the same degree of credulity, I would not have to be concerned with the names of people, only what they said *specifically* about features, or times of appearance, or habit, concerning the Monster. Before starting on this considerable task it was necessary to think about the matter of policy, and fitting the results into an overall scheme of things, without a proper understanding of which it would be easy to waste both time and energy.

Weighing up the situation carefully, I decided on the following plan, each phase of which would have to be confirmed or explained, at least to my own satisfaction, before proceeding to the next.

Plan of campaign

Phase	Fundamental questions	Action
1.	Can it possibly be real?	Study evidence and decide.
2.	Is it still alive?	Photo reconnaissance at the loch.
3.	Can it be related to any known species?	Research.
4.	Are there more than one?	Research.
5.	How can it be protected and studied effectively?	?

The first part of the plan could obviously be tackled at once, so I obtained a number of sheets of paper 40 × 20 in. across, and drew lines and columns under a string of headings, and started the laborious task of examining each report; stripping it of useful detail, then writing this in under appropriate headings—year, month, date, time of sighting, neck, head, body—and so on.

The analysis took five months to complete but by the end of it I knew a great deal more about the Monster; more than could be gleaned by simply reading books and articles about it. Slowly but surely, as the jig-saw puzzle went together a picture materialized, showing up in extraordinary detail the parts of the animal, the colour of its skin, the way it swam and dived, the astonishment of those who had seen it—and as I sat down each evening to study these reports, often working into the silent hours, like a conspirator, I enjoyed the drama of the situation. Here before me lay the clue to the first part of the puzzle, upon which depended future action; the prospect of which was really most appealing! To go and look for a legendary Monster was one thing, but to look for it in the belief it existed was quite another—and much more exciting. Suddenly the task assumed an almost hypnotic quality, and unconscious of time I laboured on, reading reports, dissecting them, then tucking the parts away into columns, the totals of which became more intelligible as the work progressed.

From the start it was quite apparent that people spoke with consistency, describing the parts of the Monster and their reactions to it in similar terms—truly remarkable consistency in all respects but one, and in that they were consistently *inconsistent*. Everyone seemed to have noted a different number of 'humps' in the water: one, two, three and even more on occasions, and sometimes no humps at all, just a huge back like an upturned boat. It was difficult to understand, but important, because it showed people were not just copying each other. Had they intended to do so, descriptions would not have varied on this one particular point. Alternatively, had they set out to be different they would have been different about several features, whereas descriptions tallied right down the line of headings; except for the 'humps' about which no one could agree.

As the analysis grew in length, and it became possible to check across the spread of years, I began to notice subtle hidden detail: odd snippets of speech describing habit and behaviour, the exact significance of which was not apparent outside the selective framework of the analysis, and I came to realize that in attempting to prove the Monster, I was proving something else as well—the honesty of people: this ample cross-section of ordinary people.

Eventually the job was done, and the picture of the Monster very clear indeed, a picture built up of ten thousand words spread across yards of paper, in orderly columns of specific statement, and from it I was able to construct a model of the beast with reasonable assurance: a creature so strange in appearance I could hardly believe the shape that developed. And yet to doubt it would be to disregard the work I had just completed—about which I no longer had any doubt at all. Thus it appeared that phase one of my plan was almost complete. On the basis of an impartial study of what many people said, the Monster *appeared* to be real: but it was still very difficult to accept. The model I had built portrayed an animal the like of which did not exist on earth—a creature with a long snake-like neck, a huge body, paddles and a tail, altogether 40, or even 50 ft in length!

Excerpts from the analysis with conclusions

Based on one hundred separate eye-witness reports, obtained over twenty-six years, from various sources: commencing May 1933, and ending September 1958.

1. *Year of appearance*
The Monster appeared consistently during this period of time, and although the great majority of reports stem from the years 1933 and 1934, there is no real significance in this fact, and it is pointless to quote statistics. In the early thirties the Monster was not considered to be a joke, and people were not afraid to speak of what they had seen. Furthermore, due to the felling of trees and construction work, more of the loch was seen by more people than ever before, or since, and in consequence, more reports were recorded.

2. *Month seen*
Statistics: January, 3 sightings; February, 4; March, 10; April, 10; May, 7; June, 9; July, 14; August, 16; September, 5; October, 5; November, 6; December, 6; 'summer', 3; 'autumn', 2.

These figures are of course based on the hundred reports under consideration, and although it is plain that the Monster is seen all the year round, no firm conclusion can be drawn as to when it most commonly appears.

In winter, the loch is viewed almost exclusively by the local population, who rarely speak of the Monster even if they see it. In summertime, there are visitors in hundreds, but the leaves are on the trees, and along two-thirds of the roads surrounding the loch it is not possible to see the water; in winter it is, in places. It is variables of this kind which invalidate the figures quoted above, but there *is* evidence to suggest the Monster has a preference for sunshine, or, more properly perhaps, warm water. In summer the water on the surface of the loch is several degrees warmer than that below, so—taking everything into consideration, it appears that summer months are probably best for viewing.

3.   *Time of day*
Statistics: 85 per cent of surface appearances occur between dawn and 9.30 a.m.

This characteristic is quite clear, and important for two reasons. From a zoological point of view, it suggests the presence of a nocturnal animal, and from a practical viewpoint it provides a definite period of time each day, during which the odds against seeing it are reduced. It is, however, occasionally seen at all times throughout the day as well.

4.   *The head and neck*
Statistics: described in 43 per cent of recorded sightings.

The following descriptive excerpts are but a few of many:

A horse-like head with a long neck—serpent-like head, diameter not greater than neck—long undulating neck, slightly thicker than an elephant's trunk—head the size of a cow's, but flatter, visible neck about five feet long and one foot thick—head and face the size of a large dog, but definitely, snake-like—face like a goat, two stumps on top of head like sheep's horns broken off—eyes like slits in a darning needle—flat reptilian head, which it shook vigorously from side to side—head hardly wider than neck in profile, turned together from side to side—eyes large and glittering—like a huge swan with body submerged—Monster with huge long neck rose from the water—etc., etc.

The comparisons made with the heads of other animals inevitably differ to some extent, but if the matter of profile is given due consideration, they are not so much at variance after all. The majority of descriptions seem to refer to a possibly reptilian type of head though modified to include a snout and a most curious pair of 'horns' or protrusions occasionally seen on top of the head, exactly like those of a giraffe or a snail. The reported size of the head varies from one account to the next also, but it should be remembered that, over water, both distance and scale are very hard to judge.

On occasions, white markings have been observed on the throat and cheeks. The mouth has been estimated at 12–18 in. in width, and has been watched opening and closing every two seconds or so, as though the animal was breathing; and once, 'a kind of steam' was seen to issue from its mouth, and was blown back by the wind.

The most pronounced characteristic of the head is that it is *tiny* in relation to the enormous body to which it belongs and in profile it is hardly thicker than the neck itself: indeed, some witnesses fail to distinguish the head, as it seems no more than an extension of the neck, but those that do, at close quarters, all seem to agree that it is very ugly—flat on top, and usually without evidence of eyes. When the eyes *are* seen they are said to be like slits, near the top of the head, although they are occasionally referred to as being very large indeed, and glittering or luminescent. But whatever the most fitting description may be, one thing appears to be certain, they are not the eyes of a fish.

All things considered, the head of the animal is of particular zoological interest and importance, and no less the neck, which exhibits equally puzzling characteristics. When the head and neck break surface they are usually carried at an angle of 30 degrees or so to the water, when the animal is moving at any speed, and only a foot or two may be showing, but on other occasions the neck protrudes at a very upright angle, the line of which is carried on by the head, rather in the fashion of an outraged farmyard gander, stretching its neck while hissing in defiance. In this position, which is by no means unusual, the neck is often described as a 'black pillar', or pole-like object streaking through the water, with spray breaking from it very much as it does from the bows of a ship. Estimates of height above the water are commonly 5–6 ft and the thickness is generally thought to be about a foot; but it tapers towards the head and at the other extremity where it joins the massive body, it thickens very suddenly.

Occasionally the neck emerges slowly from the water, without any visible indication of the body behind it, and in this position the head and neck present a graceful almost swan-like appearance,

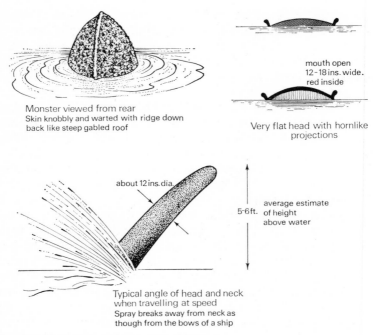

Monster viewed from rear
Skin knobbly and warted with ridge down
back like steep gabled roof

mouth open
12-18 ins. wide.
red inside

Very flat head with hornlike
projections

about 12 ins. dia.

5-6 ft.

average estimate
of height
above water

Typical angle of head and neck
when travelling at speed
Spray breaks away from neck as
though from the bows of a ship

Figure 1   Some impressions of the Monster.

and people comment on its poise and balance. On several occasions, the head has been seen to turn rapidly from side to side 'as quick as a hen' or to shake itself vigorously, giving the appearance of acute awareness both of sight and sound; and there is evidence to suggest the latter sense may in fact be well developed. There must be at least a dozen recorded accounts which suggest the animal reacts immediately to sound—to a shouted exclamation, or the noise of a motor-boat engine, causing it to dive at once.

Taking into account the angle at which the neck is held, or the graceful arch when motionless in the water, and the consistent reference to a height of 5–6 ft above the water, total length of the neck must be 9 or 10 ft, and in view of its sinuous flexible movements it must be extremely muscular; a solid pillar of muscle springing from a tremendous breadth of shoulder, 2 or 3 ft thick at its base perhaps, then tapering down suddenly before continuing out to the head with an almost parallel thickness.

It is a very remarkable neck and if people are to be believed it is quite unlike that of any known *living species*—fish, mammal, amphibian or reptile, and there is no doubt that irrefutable proof of its existence will provide a very tough morsel for scientists to chew upon.

5.   *The mane*

Statistics: reference is made to a mane, or neck frill of some sort, in 5 per cent of sightings.

It seems just too much to expect that the fabulous 'water horse' should exhibit a mane in addition to its other astonishing features, but if reports are studied impartially, there does appear to be some sort of appendage attached behind the head and neck which is quite distinct when seen, though it is not often reported; but perhaps this can be explained by the fact the animal is so rarely seen at close quarters.

On different occasions the mane has been described in the following words:

like a small frill on top of the neck—saw something like hair or wool on the back of the neck.—Something extended 4 ft down the back of the neck from the head; dark coloured, rather like a mane.—The head and neck seemed to be covered with some sort of entangling substance.—At the back of the neck there was a curious fin.

If we are to believe reports at all, we must not accept only those which fit the 'conventional' (if that is the word to use) pattern of sightings, and discard the others which do not. Each report must be carefully studied and with regard to the mane in particular this principle must stand.

For the moment therefore it is well to remain content with a temporary acceptance of what appears to be highly improbable, recalling to mind the fact that a 'frill' is displayed on the neck and back of some of the larger lizards. The iguana for example, and the ancient tuatara of New Zealand, both of which, of course, belong to the reptile family.

6.   *The body*

Statistics: in 20 per cent of sightings, a back or body is reported as distinct from the appearance of humps, and the most common description is that of 'an upturned boat', but others have said: 'It looked like an elephant's back—stood about 4 ft high and 10–12 ft in length—an egg-shaped body—seen end on there is a distinct angle at apex of back—a long dark body—like a gigantic eel 25 ft in length and 5 ft in diameter.'

Descriptions such as these are not very specific and the best that can be said for them is that the majority refer to some very large object.

7.   *The humps*

Statistics: 'humps' appear in no less than 45 per cent of sightings, but these must be subdivided because the number of humps vary in quite an extraordinary manner. From amongst these forty-five separate statements, eight refer to one hump, nineteen to two, nine to three, and the remainder to a varied number of humps or 'coils' up to a counted total of twelve! At first sight it does not seem possible to explain this part of the riddle, and it is as well not to try—not until the subject has been studied in much greater detail, but it can do no harm to assess the size and shape of these remarkable protuberances.

Generally speaking, there appears to be three basic triangular humps, the largest in the middle, standing 3–4 ft above the surface, 5–6 ft in length at the water line, and separated by 6–8 ft of clear water from the other two humps. This adds up to an overall visible length of 30 ft or so. The humps, when seen, appear to be quite definitely structural and solid, like a 'steep-gabled house'. The angle subtended is almost a right angle, and when viewed in this position it seems that they cannot possibly relate directly to the backbone. They are not vertical undulations, and they are not fins. Probably the only certain thing about them is that they are most peculiar, and a complete stumbling block to science. No known animal is capable of producing such a body shape—but the mystery does not end here.

The evidence states quite clearly that the humps vary in number, shape and size, and that on occasions these changes have actually been watched taking place! Sometimes rounded humps are seen, instead of triangles and then again a whole collection of minor humps in a row; and the animal has been seen to swim off with three humps clearly in evidence and then return a few minutes later with no visible humps at all.

Unbelievable though it may seem, there can be little doubt that the visible parts of the *back* of the animal are capable of changing shape.

8.   *Limbs, fins or paddles*

Statistics: mentioned in 13 per cent of sightings.

In the majority of cases only the splashes are noted, but on

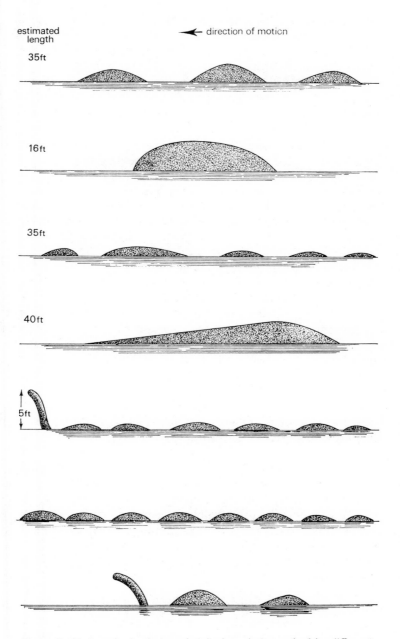

Figure 2 Various body shapes sketched or photographed by different observers.

three occasions the forward flippers have been actually seen out of the water, by different people.

This is a matter of considerable zoological importance, and if it is possible to establish beyond doubt that the animal has flippers or paddles instead of legs it may help to lessen the doubt about its identity or the original species to which it is related. This is an important point, but recorded descriptions are not always clear.

> Saw front paddles working alternately as it turned about—
> saw what might have been limbs or flippers beating the
> water—saw two fore flippers extended but not being moved—
> considered there was evidence of paddling movement fore
> and aft and on either side—short legs or flippers—the wash
> was generated from a point behind the head and again from
> behind the second hump, as if powerful flippers were at
> work.

Verbal reports like these are not sufficiently explicit and more concrete evidence must first be obtained before the matter is decided, but from what people have said it appears probable the Monster uses flippers or paddles to propel it through the water, and furthermore that the rear pair are larger than those at the front.

9.   *The tail*
Statistics: reported in 11 per cent of sightings.

Descriptions of a tail are relatively few in number, but are generally quite specific; for example:

> I saw the tail distinctly causing a great commotion, thrashing
> the water with much force—tail thrashed water like a
> propeller—he thought that a powerful tail could be seen
> moving from side to side below the surface—commotion in
> water about 15–20 ft behind last hump—two humps came
> into view and the whole length of tail could be seen on the
> surface, he judged the Monster to be 18–20 ft long, the tail
> being about 6 ft long.

The presence of a tail is also of great interest, and so is the fact that it appears to be used in swimming. On one occasion only has it actually been seen out of the water, and on that occasion the estimate of length coincided with that recorded above—6 ft;

but in both instances the animal was thought to be no more than 20 ft in length overall, and as so many estimates of size suggest another very much bigger animal lives in the loch, it would be reasonable to expect its tail to be rather longer. In the second-last excerpt recorded above, a commotion was noticed 15–20 ft behind the *last hump*, an estimate that compares with several other reports.

10. *Size or length*
In no less than 33 per cent of sightings specific reference is made to size, and in the graphic words used in these reports it is possible to gain some impression of the enormous bulk of body.

Estimated 40 ft in length was showing—great size and bulk; length about 30 ft—huge creature about 30 ft in length—tremendous creature—tremendously long dark object—full 30 ft—it was a really huge creature—it was very great—must be of huge proportions—30 to 40 ft of it, etc.

It is true to say that distance and scale are very difficult to judge correctly over water, but people have seen the animal, on occasions, at a distance of but a few yards, and there is no doubt at all that it is very, very large indeed—quite literally a Monster!

11. *Colour*
Specific reference 28 per cent.
From amongst these reports two colours are reported consistently—elephant or battleship grey, and reddish brown; both these colours are referred to with equal frequency and in quite definite terms.

A few people have said the Monster is an olive green, a greenish black, black, or just dark in appearance, but in the latter case poor light, distance, or shadows may have obscured the true colour to some extent. There is some evidence to suggest that there may be a whitish strip down the throat, and in one instance white marks were seen on the 'cheeks' of the face at a distance of no more than 40 yards. Beneath the water line the colour of the body is sometimes said to be lighter than those parts showing above, but taking a cross-section of all these reports one can only conclude the animal is either able to change colour at will, or that colour varies with age or sex. The ability to change colour is characteristic of reptiles, but as no one has actually seen this happening, it seems more probable that the two most usual colours, brown and grey, have something to do with age or sex. A live crocodile, swimming in the water, could fittingly be described as greenish black, with lighter underparts, but to make comparisons of this sort may well be misleading, and the issue cannot be decided until a clear sequence of colour film is obtained at relatively close quarters.

12.   *Skin or scales*
Specific reference 15 per cent. *None* of these reports refer to scales, and of those that mention texture about half say the skin appears smooth or glistening and the other half say it is rough, like that of a toad, or an elephant:

> Loathsome texture, reminiscent of a snail—rough looking— tough looking—skin dark and glistening—not smooth— like that of an elephant—not hairy—not glossy—skin glistening and fairly smooth—hide was something like that of an elephant or an immense toad, etc.

The one thing about which all these reports agree is that it is *skin*, but bearing in mind the effects that light and shade, wetness and dryness could have on any surface viewed at a distance, it would be well to reserve judgment about texture. But at the same time there is one valid argument which suggests the skin may in fact be rough rather than smooth: a rough wet surface seen at a distance with the sun shining on it might appear shiny, and therefore smooth, whereas a smooth surface, wet or dry, would never appear rough.

It is perhaps too easy to draw a parallel between the 'toad-like' appearance of the skin and the many reptiles that possess this sort of covering. Although, on the face of it, it is conceivable that it may turn out to be a reptile, one might be equally inclined to call it an amphibian, or even a mammal, on the strength of similar comparisons made with an elephant's hide. Again, there is really not enough evidence on which to base conclusions, but the little that exists suggests a tough or warty hide on the body only. The neck is invariably reported as being smooth, and shining when wet.

13.   *Human reaction*
The information contained under this heading is difficult to analyse unless one is prepared to include a 'factor' for astonish-

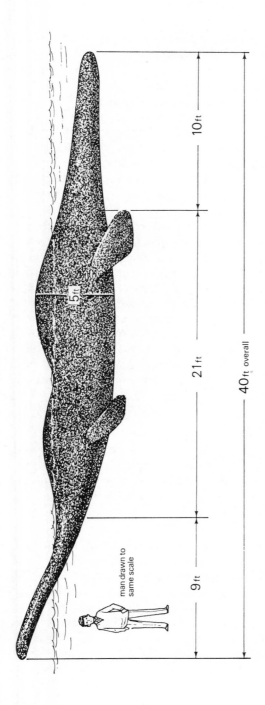

Figure 3   An impression of the Monster based on average statistics, showing the two humps most commonly reported.

ment, because in this column people's reactions have been noted carefully, and these are some of the comments made:

> Fantastic creature—the most extraordinary form of animal—appearance like a huge caterpillar (multi-hump position)—marvellous sight—remarkable creature—huge creature in a fury, lashed about—strange creature—a most amazing beast—like a monster of prehistoric times—petrified with astonishment—never seen anything like it before—an amazing sight—like a prehistoric monster in a school book—an astonishing sight quite unlike anything I have ever seen, etc.

If these are false impressions—lies—there must be many liars, but from amongst the mass of more usual evidence human reaction can also be measured in terms different to those of mere astonishment. At a distance, people are sometimes awestruck by what they see: the very strangeness of the Monster, the graceful way in which it rides the waters of the loch, its size and amazing turn of speed all combine to present a picture so entirely different to anything before experienced, that those who witness it are much affected. At really close quarters this sense of awe is sometimes turned to one of fear, and of the relatively few people who have seen the beast at really close quarters, some are not ashamed to admit to being very much afraid.

14. *Speed*

In 37 per cent of reports people make some reference to speed, and the majority state the Monster is capable of almost unbelievable speed—but it is also fond of lolling or basking on the surface, and has been watched enjoying itself in this manner for periods of up to forty minutes.

> Cruising along at 20–30 m.p.h.—motionless for 10 minutes—swimming at a furious rate—loafing in the water—lay basking on the surface—terrific speed like a motor boat—slow moving, then suddenly dashed forward with incredible speed—kept pace with the Monster at 25 m.p.h. in my car—had never seen anything travel on water so fast, it streaked across the loch—speed about 35 m.p.h.—tremendous speed—faster than a fast motor boat—racing through water at terrific speed, etc.

Reading these accounts in greater detail, two other characteristics come to light: the animal is inclined to 'dash' off suddenly,
and when it does, it travels dead straight or in a gentle curve, but
when it is paddling slowly, it often zigzags about as if undeter-
mined where to go. Furthermore, if accounts of great speed are
to be believed it must possess enormous strength and a very good
hydrodynamic shape, allowing its great bulk to slip through the
water with minimum resistance.

15. *Wash or wake*
Statistics: 44 per cent reference.
As might be expected almost every other report refers to the
wash the animal creates.

V-shaped wash in straight line at speed of outboard motor-
boat—big splash—churning mass of white foam—parting
water from its neck like a motor-boat—V-shaped wash;
disturbance like that from a small ship—turmoil of water,
miniature tidal wave—terrific commotion—leaving wake
like that from a torpedo—sending up waves like a speed
boat—waves like a steamer—big V wash, clearly visible at
1,800 yards—tremendous streak of white foam—an area 400
yards in diameter in turmoil—wash like a powerful speed
boat, etc.

Disturbances like these would never be made by a small
animal—on the contrary, they suggest the presence of something
quite extraordinarily large and powerful.

16. *Dive or submergence*
Statistics: 25 per cent reference.
In reading reports about the Monster it is apparent there is
something very odd about the way it disappears—something very
odd indeed, so strange in fact it warrants the closest study, and if
the remarks recorded under this heading appear repetitive, they
are none the less worth noticing because they clearly prove a
point which is of great significance. The Monster, though capable
of diving in the manner that might be expected of it, head and
neck first, followed by the body—only does so when suddenly
frightened. Statistics show that in 88 per cent of noted dis-
appearances it *sinks vertically*, almost without a ripple:

It turned sharply and sank—disappeared—then sank—it sank—
then it sank—sank instantaneously—*dived* immediately when
boats appeared—it sank down slowly as a whole, the relative
position of head and neck remained unchanged—gradually
sank—turned sharply, as though startled by the shouting
and *plunged* beneath the water—sank perpendicularly—
lowered its long neck and *dived* (on hearing approach of
herring drifters)—it sank quite suddenly—submerged
perpendicularly.

In assessing these many similar statements, there can be no
doubt that the Monster is able to sink straight down at will; and
very rapidly too. This is quite extraordinary, and can only be
explained in one of three ways. Either it forces its buoyant body
underwater by displacing water upwards with its flippers, *or*, it
alters its specific gravity—the density of its flesh and bones, *or*,
it alters its actual displacement—by getting bigger or smaller.

The first possibility can certainly be ruled out, because it 'sinks
without a ripple', and the second is very hard to conceive, but
the third provides a ready answer, and fits nicely into place when
the facts are considered—the facts of the variable number of
humps, and the ability to visibly alter shape.

17.   *Amphibious appearances on shore*
The animal has been reported wholly or partly clear of the water
on at least seven separate occasions, and there seems little reason
to doubt the truth of statements. The most important thing about
them is that they suggest the presence of an air-breathing animal
of some sort because on one occasion the Monster was reported
clear of the water for twenty-five minutes.

Quite clearly, it is these strange accounts of the Monster
actually out of the water on the shores of the loch which must be
studied closest of all, because in them we can expect to find
descriptive detail concerning parts of the animal never seen when
swimming in the water.

18.   *Time spent on surface*
Reports vary considerably.

In most cases the animal is seen swimming on the surface, for
between five and ten minutes, but on occasions it has remained
visible for up to forty minutes and sometimes longer. Very rare

though its surface appearances certainly are, when it *does* show up it seems to like to splash about or bask in the sunshine.

19. *Place of appearance*
A dozen or so authenticated appearances have been plotted on the map shown on page 65. These represent but a fraction of the hundreds of sightings recorded, and an even smaller proportion of those that are not: which must be numbered in thousands, if due regard is given to the fact that only a small minority of reports ever find their way into print.

Looking at the crosses on the map, two things are apparent—the Monster is seen in all parts of the loch, from one end to the other, and the most common places noted are opposite populated areas. It is this second fact which is of significance.

If people were telling lies about seeing a Monster they would probably not say they had seen it outside their own homes—in Foyers bay, or immediately off Fort Augustus, for example, where most of the crosses are bunched together just off shore; on the contrary, they would probably claim to have seen it in some remote part of the loch; but on looking at the map, the remote parts of the loch are almost devoid of crosses.

This is an important point, and implies that people are telling the truth.

20. *Viewing conditions*
Under this heading, conditions of visibility, wind and water are noted, but it is pointless to attempt to analyse the very many reports, which vary from one extreme to the other. On some occasions the Monster has been seen only a few yards off in broad daylight, without a breath of wind, swimming on the glassy surface of the loch, and on others it has been watched a mile or so away, buffeting its way through rough water in poor visibility; but under all conditions, those who claim to have seen it appear to be entirely sure of the fact they really have seen it, and have not been fooled by some commonplace object, like a tree trunk bobbing about in the water.

Perhaps this assurance is more understandable, when reading an account in *More than a Legend* in which two young observers watched the Monster at a range of some 3,500 yards and reported they could see it quite distinctly at this distance with the naked eye! If this report is true the animal must be of a size that puts it outside the category of any known freshwater species—and thus it remains a complete enigma; but from out of this analysis it is possible to construct a picture of the beast which gains its shape and form from the words of a hundred different people.

The outline of this picture, therefore, cannot reasonably be so very far from the truth.

3 Fable and fact

For the very earliest recorded account of the Monster, it is necessary to turn back the pages of time, and translate directly from a Latin text, and for this a debt of thanks is due to Father J. A. Carruth, monk at St Benedict's, the peaceful abbey at Fort Augustus at the south-western end of the loch, in whose concise little booklet *Loch Ness and its Monster* a tale is recorded as follows:

Proof from History: The following account is from the trustworthy Latin life of the great St Columba, the Abbot of Iona, written by St Adamnan, who later himself became Abbot of Iona. In his introduction to the life of the saint, Adamnan, himself a man whom the Venerable Bede calls 'A good and wise man, and very well instructed in the lore of the scriptures' writes as follows:

'Let no one imagine that I either state a falsehood regarding so great a man, or record anything doubtful or uncertain. Be it known that I will tell with all candour what I have learned from the consistent narrative of my predecessors, trustworthy and discerning men, and that my narrative is founded either on what I have been able to find recorded in the pages of those who have gone before me, or what I have learned on diligent inquiry, by hearing it from certain faithful old men, who told me without hesitation.'

The date of the following occurrence narrated by Adamnan is about A.D. 565 and from Book 2, chapter 27, of his biography of St Columba.

'OF THE DRIVING AWAY OF A CERTAIN WATER MONSTER BY VIRTUE OF PRAYER OF THE HOLY MAN.—At another time, again when the blessed man was staying for some days in the province of the Picts, he found it necessary to cross the river Ness; and when he came to the bank thereof, he sees some of the inhabitants burying a poor unfortunate man, whom, as those who were burying him themselves reported, some water monster had, a little before, snatched at as he was swimming and bitten with a most savage bite, and whose

hapless corpse some men who came in a boat to give
assistance, though too late, caught hold of by putting out
hooks. The blessed man, however, on hearing this, directs
that some one of his companions shall swim out and
bring to him the boat that is on the other side, sailing it
across. On hearing this direction of the holy and famous
man, Lugne Mocumin, obeying without delay, throws off
all his clothes except his undergarment, and casts himself
into the water. Now the Monster, which was not so much
satiated as made eager for prey, was lying hid in the bottom
of the river; but perceiving that the water above was disturbed
by him who was crossing, suddenly emerged, and swimming
to the man as he was crossing in the middle of the stream,
rushed up with a great roar and open mouth.

'Then the Blessed man looked on, while all who were
there, the heathen as well as the brethren, were stricken with
very great terror; and with his holy hand raised on high he
formed the sign of the cross in the empty air, invoked the
name of God, and commanded the fierce monster, saying,—
Think not to go further nor touch thou that man. Quick go
back! Then the beast on hearing this voice of the saint, was
terrified and fled backwards more rapidly than he came, as if
dragged by cords, although it had come so near to Lugne
as he swam, that there was not more than the length of a
punt pole between the man and the beast. Then the
brethren, seeing that the beast had gone away and that their
comrade Lugne was returned to them safe and sound in the
boat, glorified God in the blessed man, greatly marvelling.
Moreover also the barbarous heathen who were there present,
constrained by the greatness of the miracle, which they
themselves had seen, glorified the God of the Christians.'

This very strange account of a Monster is worth the closest
study, for it contains features consistent with reports from
the present day, though in one it differs entirely. At no time
since has there ever been another reported example of the animal
attacking a man in the water, but if it can be established the
account is only partly true, it would perhaps be a mistake to rule
out this unpleasant possibility; indeed there is a sinister saying
at Loch Ness in which many still believe, that the loch 'never
gives up its dead'.

Returning again to the account; it is known that Adamnan

wrote his biography some hundred years after the event he describes so vividly, but considering the fame of St Columba, there is little doubt the story of his life and teachings remained faithfully recorded in the minds of many followers, and judging by the extraordinary nature of this particular event, it is reasonable to expect that details of it would remain clear, long after less exciting memories had died.

Furthermore, a careful study of the process by which legends are formed* has shown that the memory of historical detail tends to continue for at least five or six generations among communities that have no written language—150 years on average—and thus assuming no written record was made at the time, the story might well have survived without undue distortion on a purely verbal basis; but Adamnan claims he relied at least in part on written evidence.

The case for the original therefore appears to be fairly sound, and once recorded, the truth owes nothing to the passage of time.

Looking at the substance of the story now with greater confidence, there are certain points that immediately strike those familiar with reports about the Monster. To begin with, Adamnan protests he only writes the truth or what he understands to be the truth. This protestation of good faith is perhaps the most noticeable characteristic of those who have seen or heard tell of the Monster, and dare to talk about it. Modern reports show this quite clearly.

Next, we should consider the presence of a water monster in the river Ness, or more correctly Nesa, the name by which the river was known in ancient time. It can be no mere coincidence this fearsome creature appeared before St Columba at this particular place, amongst all the lochs and rivers of Scotland, or that the brethren were 'stricken with very great terror' at what they saw, because, as later reports will show, of the few people at Loch Ness today who have seen the animal at very close quarters, some have expressed a natural fear of it, and in one or two cases even admit to an undignified retreat, which perhaps is not a reaction of which to be ashamed.

On the reappearance of the Monster and its approach to the valiant fellow, clad only in an undergarment, swimming in the water: 'the Blessed man looked on ... and with his holy hand raised on high . . . commanded the fierce monster, saying—Think not

---

* Van Gennep, quoted in Dr Bernard Heuvelmans, *On the Track of Unknown Animals* (London: Rupert Hart-Davis, 1958), p. 82.

to go further nor touch that man. Quick go back! Then the beast on hearing this voice of the saint, was terrified and fled backwards more rapidly than he came, as if dragged by cords . . .'

Now St Columba, it is known, had a powerful voice with which he taught his Christian faith to the warlike men of the Highlands, and the Monster, it is known, reacts immediately to sound, diving at once when frightened. Modern men and women too have shouted in excitement, or fear, when surprised by the creature, and on each, as records show, it has disappeared from sight.

It would of course be wise to allow some poetic licence in the telling of this tale, apparent, no doubt, in reference to the beast as it rushed towards the man 'with a great roar and open mouth', because as far as is known the Monster of today has no voice at all, though it *has* been seen to open and close its mouth—but whatever the truth of it is, there can be little doubt that this early report, recorded so many centuries ago, contains information of most unusual interest—and may even be reasonably accurate. If it is, and if the Monster of today can be proved to be real, those who choose to swim in the loch may do so at their peril.

The next report of the Monster is of much later origin and is but one of several legendary excerpts and stories recorded by Mrs Whyte, who has done much useful research on the subject. In 1527 or thereabouts a certain Duncan Campbell's experience was recounted as follows:*

This terrible beast—issuing out of the water early one morning about mid summer, he did very easily and without any force or straining of himself overthrow huge oaks with his tail and therewith killed outright three men that hunted him with three strokes of his tail, the rest of them saving themselves in trees thereabouts, whilst the aforesaid monster returned to the loch.

Fanciful though this account may at first appear, like that of St Columba's day, there are, once more, features in it consistent with modern reports obtained from reliable sources. If this is pure coincidence it is indeed remarkable, because within the scope of those few lines written centuries ago, descriptive phrases appear which fit the theoretical picture of the Monster

* Hector Boece, *History of Scotland*.

of today—a picture built up on strength of analysis four hundred years after the event referred to! Once more the animal is described as a 'terrible beast'; words that convey a sense of fear or superstitious dread; and it is said to have climbed out of the water on to dry land, one early morning, and to have switched its tail about with astonishing effect.

Another more recent though equally delightful passage from monster history is recorded in the Chronicle of Fortingall which printed the following account in 1870:

> There was ane monstrous fish seen in Lochfyne, having great in the head thereof, and at times waed stand aboon the water as high as the mast of a ship; and the said had upon the head thereof twa croons . . .

At this time in Scottish history the legend of the fabled 'water horse' was strong in several different Highland lochs, and continued through the years. It gained strength as communications slowly improved and remote areas came more within the range of travellers, to whom, in previous centuries, this craggy part of Scotland must have appeared as remote as part of the moon itself.

Continuing the search for other signs of Monster lore, it is necessary to refer to some very early maps. In her chapter 'The Highlander and the Water Horse' Mrs Whyte draws attention to a Latin inscription found on a map dated 1325–50, held in the Bodleian Library, in reference to Loch Tay, and again another in Blaens Atlas of 1635 on which a similar note appears, referring to Loch Lomond: 'Waves without wind, fish without fin, and a floating island' and then an explanatory note—'the fish they speak of as having no fins are a kind of snake, and therefore no wonder!' These are very quaint remarks, emerging from the shadows of the past, and perhaps it is too easy to see in statements such as these meanings that do not exist. But if the Monster is real at all, the people who saw it, or its antecedents, swimming about two or three hundred years ago might reasonably be expected to describe it in whatever terms appeared most fitting to them at the time. Although it is true to say that none of these remarks refers directly to Loch Ness, it should be made clear at once that evidence exists for monsters seen in other lochs today, though not in Tay or Lochfyne. For example: in the western coastal regions of the Highlands, at both Loch Shiel and Loch Morar recent evidence can be found which is at least as convincing as that for Loch Ness itself, and in half a dozen other lochs there is a weighty legendary history—but this is digressing to some extent.

In the latter part of the last century, reports of the Monster in Loch Ness began to come in from various sources with consistency of detail, but those that were recorded were few in number, and caused no particular interest outside the Highlands. Understandably, perhaps, zoologists and men of science, remote in more respects than one, simply did not believe them. The century turned, and the years rolled by and the stories remained of purely local interest and belief—and then in the early thirties plans were put in hand for a motor road to run along the northern shore of the Loch. When construction started in 1933, it introduced the flood of 'modern' sightings, to which reference has already been made; but these first early reports seem to have had little effect on scientists, few of whom ventured to the loch—preferring it seems to reserve judgment until more definite evidence was obtained. Others openly adopted a cynical attitude, treating the whole business as a joke or mass hallucination, publishing statements to this effect and, in so doing, demonstrating a scant regard for fact, or the balanced reports of so many people, who stood to gain nothing by making them.

Then, on 22 July of that year a most extraordinary thing happened, so extraordinary it taxed the imagination of even the most confirmed believers.

Driving down the narrow road, early one morning, between the village of Dores and Inverfarigaig, a Mr Spicer and his wife saw 'a most extraordinary form of animal' crossing the road ahead: which at this point lay some 20 yards from the water. First a long neck appeared, undulating rapidly, forming a number of arches.

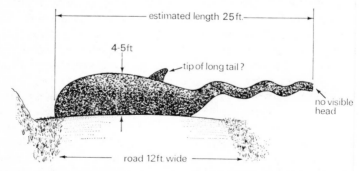

Figure 4   The animal described by Mr and Mrs Spicer, seen crossing the road near Dores, 22 July 1933.

It was a little thicker than an elephant's trunk, and stretched the width of the road, and behind it a huge ponderous body, lurched ungainly towards the loch. In seconds it crossed the road, and disappeared through the bushes out of sight. The Spicers, at first some 200 yards distant, accelerated towards it; but when they arrived there was nothing to see, just a gap in the undergrowth through which the creature must have passed. They heard no splash, but the noise of the engine might well have drowned it; neither did they see any limbs, but the creature's lower extremities were obscured by a dip in the road, which at this place was some 10 to 12 ft in width. The animal's body was about 4 ft high and together with the neck, about 25 ft in length.

Staggered, and curiously repelled by what they had seen, the Spicers withstood the barrage of questions shot at them after the event by various interested people, one of whom had come to the loch especially to investigate—Commander R. T. Gould, R.N., famous for his analytical studies and books on unusual subjects. Gould was a man of undoubted brilliance and integrity and his opinion could only have been based on a carefully objective study of the story, and the people who told it, and he came out unreservedly on the side of the Spicers. He believed they were telling the truth and had 'undergone a most unusual experience'. Certainly this was borne out by the Spicers' description, and their willingness to take 'an oath or make any affidavit' in support of it.

The effect this extraordinary story had on the affairs of the Monster is hard to judge, for the time of high excitement had yet to come, but it is probable the news of this almost nightmarish experience adversely affected scientific opinion—for enough was enough, by any standard, and descriptions of a Monster *in* the Loch were more than most could swallow; but as the year wore on, and reports came in by the hundred, popular interest blossomed on an international scale, bringing with it the inevitable tide of spectators. Huge prizes were offered for the animal dead or alive; but preferably alive. Bertram Mills pledged a sum of £20,000 to any man who would deliver the creature alive to the circus—but to no avail. In spite of these inducements, the public found it difficult enough to photograph the Monster, let alone catch it; though there were indeed a number of enterprising schemes for netting the loch, electrifying it, or draining it; but none came to maturity. The size of the place defied all practicable attempts to catch the elusive beast, but in November of 1933 a photograph *was* obtained, perhaps the first ever to be taken.

One Sunday morning, an employee of the British Aluminium Company works at Foyers, a Mr Hugh Gray, was taking a leisurely stroll along the narrow footpath leading away from the village, in a westerly direction, about 30 ft above the shore of the loch. It was quiet and peaceful, the water like glass, when suddenly, about a hundred yards off shore he saw a great upheaval of water, and then a tremendous disturbance and splashing, caused by some huge animal thrashing about. He estimated he could see about 40 ft of it—a thick rounded back, and what appeared to be a powerful tail. The visible parts protruded some three feet above the surface of the loch and remained in evidence for a minute or two, and then sank out of sight; but not before Mr Gray had secured a series of snapshots with a small box camera. In due course the film was developed by a chemist in Inverness, but of the several pictures taken only one was fit for printing. It showed a sinuous shape in the water, and although light had spoiled the film to some extent a representative from Kodak later certified that the negative had not been tampered with.

When questioned closely Mr Gray said: 'I cannot give any definite opinion of size, except that it was very great—it was a dark greyish colour; the skin was glistening and appeared smooth.'

Later that year, in December, a change in attitude occurred towards the Monster, brought on by the hoax of the hippo's foot. Details of this sorrowful, though humorous affair, are treated with commendable impartiality by Mrs Whyte in her book, and it is pointless to repeat them here. It is enough to say that this one foolish prank, in all probability, put an end to official scientific interest. The hoax at first succeeded completely: it was reported seriously and at length, absorbing both the time and patience of officials, and when finally exposed it had a most pronounced effect. From that day onwards, legitimate reports and descriptions were always subject to doubt and pardonable disbelief, and the steps which might otherwise have been taken with official backing to solve the mystery, were never taken. People who had been prepared, at least, to treat the matter with an open mind, suddenly became dubious; in fact the pendulum had begun to swing the other way. Witnesses began to think twice about reporting what they had seen, fearing ridicule.

In January, the situation was in no way improved by a second astonishing account of the Monster seen on land—once more crossing the road, and although the witness again appeared to be entirely reliable, the story that eventually reached the ears of the public owed little to the apparent truth of his original statement; adding to the doubt and despondency beginning to accumulate about the loch, the Monster, and all connected with it.

At 1 a.m. on 5 January 1934, a Mr Grant was returning home from Inverness on a motor-cycle, through a world bathed in moonlight. Nearing Abriachan, on the north eastern shore of the Loch, he suddenly noticed something large in the shadows at the right-hand side of the road. As he drew closer, he saw what he took to be a small head, turned towards him, then some huge creature with a long neck, taking fright, lurched across the road, moving diagonally away from him; it crashed through the undergrowth and disappeared into the Loch with a tremendous splash. Grant jumped off his machine, with which he had almost struck the animal, and gave chase, but by the time he had reached the water's edge only ripples remained.

Both Gould and Mrs Whyte provide a comprehensive record of this account but for the purpose of this historical summary, it is only necessary to quote Mr Grant as follows: 'Knowing something of natural history, I can say that I have never seen anything in my life like the animal I saw. It looked like a hybrid.'

Briefly his account described a creature 15–20 ft in length, with a small head like that of an eel or snake, on a long neck. The head, he thought, reached 6 ft above the ground and had large oval eyes near the crown. The rounded body had massive hind quarters and an almost kangaroo-like tail, rounded at the end, 5–6 ft in length. There appeared to be two sets of flippers,

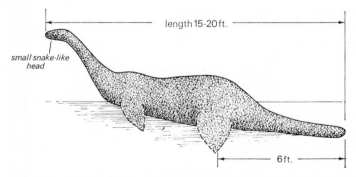

Figure 5   An impression of the animal seen by Mr Grant near Abriachan at 1.30 a.m., 5 January 1934 (shape of limbs indefinite).

which the animal used alternately in pairs in the manner of a sea lion, arching its back as it projected its bulk across the road at remarkable speed.

Later on, Mr Grant's story became embellished to some extent, with accounts of toe-marks on the shore, and heaps of animal bones—presumably the remains of a meal the Monster was supposed to have eaten! But although (like the Spicers') his original description appeared to be truthful, the effect the popular version had on the minds of scientific people can only be imagined. But his was not the only strange account to appear in 1934. In April of that same year something happened of particular significance. A man obtained a clear photograph of the head and neck of the Monster, using a quarter-plate camera and a good telephoto lens. The result was electrifying.

The man himself was a London surgeon, and his forthright testimony seemed to be above suspicion. He claimed to have obtained the picture early one morning as he drove towards Inverness along the new road along the northern shore. Once again it seemed to be purely a matter of chance: the camera had been on loan to him, and he was on the road at this unaccustomed hour because he had driven up through the night from the south and arriving too early in Fort Augustus for breakfast, had decided to motor on towards Inverness. Driving along unconcerned, he had stopped to look at a commotion in the water some 200–300 yards from the shore—when the Monster's head and neck suddenly emerged, giving him time to adjust his camera and take a total of four plates; which were later developed, with extreme care, by a reputable chemist in Inverness. The whole account, step by step, appeared perfectly believable and the sincerity of the photographer could not be questioned. And yet, when the picture was published in the *Daily Mail*, it started heated discussions and arguments that were to go on inconclusively over the next thirty-eight years.

The picture portrayed the impossible (plate 1), or something that by accepted zoological standards appeared to be impossible —the small head and serpentine neck of some large animal unknown to science, arching gracefully above the water, in silhouette—and below it the wash and counter wash of the ripples it had caused. No parts of the body could be seen clearly, but the animal's neck, frozen in an instant of time by the camera shutter, conveyed a marked impression of proportion, and balance; although completely unusual in appearance, it did somehow not appear to be *unnatural*. Perhaps the impression of grace and muscular power and the curiously attentive cant of the head stilled the tongues of critics, and certain it is there were few who openly dared to call the picture a fake, but equally few were those prepared to admit to its significance. Once more the majority of scientists preferred not to take an open stand or publish their opinions. Time rolled by lessening the interest and thought that had first centred about the picture, committing it, if not to obscurity, to a place scarcely deserved amongst the confusing mass of other evidence soon to be almost forgotten, or brushed aside with a smirk by the uninformed majority.

On 5 June 1934, another event of importance occurred, but it was given little publicity at the time and very probably did not affect the issue to any marked degree—for a number of reasons. The witness on this occasion was a maid, a native of Fort Augustus, recently employed in the service of a Mr and Mrs Pimley who lived at Kilchumein lodge, close to the Abbey turbine house at the extreme western end of the loch. Very early one morning, at about 6.30 a.m., the woman happened to look out of a window facing the loch, in the direction of Borlum Bay. On the shores of the bay, on one of the few gravel fringes to be found about the loch (the shore of which is mostly nothing but a mass of tumbled rock) she saw 'the biggest animal she had ever seen in her life', at a range of about 200 yards. It lay almost clear of the water, and its visible parts were quite unlike any she had ever seen. Fortunately, she was able to find a pair of binoculars and with these studied the creature closely for twenty-five minutes or so, the time during which it remained continuously clear of the water.

Her description, though quite remarkable, was similar to those of others—'Giraffe-like neck and absurdly small head out of all proportions to the great dark grey body, skin like an elephant and two very short fore-legs or flippers.' The animal kept turning itself in the sunshine and at times arched its back in one or more humps. Eventually, it lowered its head, quietly entered the water and disappeared.

Unfortunately, due to the fact that the witness had only recently joined the household staff of her employers, and did not realize the profound significance of what she saw, she deliberately refrained from waking them—no doubt to their considerable annoyance; but in due course the Pimleys themselves examined the beach, and found a small impression and a branch that had been pressed into the gravel—but the beach, like most of those at Loch Ness, lay upon a heavy underlying shingle, on which a weighty object would leave little, if any, impression.

The fact that this account can never receive the stamp of official approval, depending as it does on the words of a solitary witness, in no way detracts from its importance. It is in fact the naive behaviour of this witness that makes her original detailed report credible.

Next in succession of important events, after a number of minor and almost totally unsuccessful private expeditions to the Loch, we come to Sir Edward Mountain's now famous attempt to solve the mystery. In July 1934 Sir Edward came to the conclusion there was more to the Monster than met the eye, or more properly the ear, perhaps. It was not, he thought, a bottle-nosed whale, a landlocked shark, a giant squid or a rotting tree-trunk, or any other of the more facile and ridiculous suggestions put forward by people who had never been to the loch, or talked to those who had seen the animal: but whatever it was, he decided to try and find out the truth about it, and arrangements were put in hand and the services of twenty men secured to watch the loch in the manner already described.

It is difficult to assess the real results of this expedition; in one respect it proved an undoubted success with five still photographs, visual sightings and a strip of 16-mm film to confirm the presence of something large, but sadly enough it went no farther than that. It was inconclusive, the vital close-up pictures were never obtained. It well may be that this sobering fact checked less ambitious expeditions, still in the planning stage.

Sir Edward Mountain's sporting effort, made at considerable personal expense, laid the foundation for future expeditions, but in so doing, perhaps, tolled a death knell for them; and certain it is that no other comparable attempt was made on the loch for a period of twenty-six years.

At about this time, Commander R. T. Gould published his findings under the title *The Loch Ness Monster and Others*,* a painstaking work based on his own experience of the study of curious phenomena, and personal contact with witnesses at the loch. In it he analysed reports with care and impartiality, and established a case for the Monster no reasonable person could

* Now regrettably in the 'rare book' category.

doubt. For some obscure reason it seems he was never accorded the credit due him for this excellent piece of research.

The year wore on, and nothing new or startling occurred. 1935 came and went and so did 1936. Public interest began to wane, though not as quickly as it had grown at first. Hitler began to dominate the international scene, and people thought of war. Suddenly it seemed, the Monster became a joke, and to many, it must be admitted, it had never seemed more than a joke! Science decided it was safer left alone. Four years had passed and no one had captured the beast, no bones or authentic tracks had been found and of the photographs obtained only one was clear, and no one could ever really *prove* that this was not a fake. Time went by, the war clouds gathered and the nation trembled, awaiting the holocaust it knew must come; when it finally swept across these islands the Navy took control of the loch and put it out of bounds to prying eyes and cameras. Of those who lived about it, few possessed the petrol or the right to motor round its shores. But, during this period of enforced retirement the Monster obstinately continued to make occasional appearances, and although very few of these have been recorded, there is one account of interest. On this occasion the animal was carefully studied through good binoculars, at close range, by a trained observer.

Early one morning in May 1943 Mr C. B. Farrel, a member of the Royal Observer Corps, on watch for enemy bombers, spotted the Monster at a range of only 250 yards. Looking through his binoculars he could see some 25–30 ft of body and a graceful neck protruding 4–5 ft above the water. He noticed the eyes particularly, which were large and prominent, and on the back of the creature's neck he could see a curious 'fin'. It appeared to be feeding and lowered its head and neck like a swan, until both were submerged, then raised them again, shaking its head vigorously. Finally, it disappeared, without diving or any visible splash —the whole body submerged without a ripple.

After the war, and until the spring of 1959 (when this story begins), accounts of the Monster continued, gaining strength and number as life returned slowly to normal and the flood of cars and motor coaches began to swirl around the loch. Some of the stories were detailed, though adding nothing new to the host of sightings that had gone before, with so little effect: but south of the border, away from Scotland, the Monster had ceased to exist. No one spoke of it or remembered much about it and to the new generations springing up, it must have seemed no more than a childhood fairy tale, half forgotten and about as real as St George's dragon.

In Scotland, however, the Monster was still a source of interest, though there were some who said it had died; but dead or alive it retained about it an aura of doubt and superstition, and that strange mythical quality which no amount of factual evidence seemed able to remove—it remained the complete enigma, the most famous unsolved mystery on earth. Yet in 1951 a new photograph appeared, proving once more it was not an imaginary creature.

Early one morning of that year, Mr Lachlan Stewart, a woodsman who worked for the Forestry Commission, arose about 6.30 to milk his cow, when he saw something large moving out in the loch. Calling out to his friend Mr Hay, who was staying at the house, he ran down quickly to the shore. In seconds Mr Hay was by his side and both watched fascinated as the huge creature approached, displaying three separate triangular humps with water showing between each; moving at a fair speed it passed within 50 yards of the shore, and it was then that Mr Stewart, who had grabbed a small box camera before he left the house, took a snapshot. A few moments later a small head and long neck appeared in front of the first hump and was held parallel to the water, occasionally dipping into it only to reappear again.

The animal was so close by now that both watchers decided to regain the cover of the trees, but the Monster turned out towards the centre of the loch, with a great splashing, swam off and then went down head first about 300 yards off shore.

Following this event, and the usual run of sightings, the next important milestone in Monster history appears in the form of an echo recording obtained by a fishing drifter en route through the loch, which forms a link in the Caledonian ship canal system, joining the firth of Lorn in the West and the Moray Firth leading out into the North Sea.

On 2 December 1954, the Peterhead drifter, *Rival III*, obtained a quite unusual graphical recording of some large object at a depth of some 480 ft—100 ft or so above the bottom—which kept pace with the drifter for half a mile. Whatever it was it did not appear to be a shoal of fish, the graphical representation of which on the chart was all too familiar to members of the crew; and in due course, when the equipment was checked independently by the makers it was found to be in first class working order.

Turning now, in conclusion, to the years 1956 and 1957, there are two last events of interest to which reference should be made in this summary.

In 1956 the British Museum (Natural History) published the following statement in its booklet *Scientific Research:*

The most famous case of the unsubmitted specimen is that of the 'Loch Ness Monster', in which the ingenuity of suggestions as to the nature of the animal concerned has been equalled only by the powers of imagination of some observers. The only scientific evidence to which the Museum can point in explanation of this phenomenon is the report, published in the *Glasgow Sunday Post* of 27th July, 1952, of some observations made with a theodolite by Mr. Andrew McAfee. At a distance of 300 yards, he saw the three dark humps which characterize the description of the 'Monster'. With his theodolite, however, he was able to observe that the humps were shadows, and that they remained stationary while the ripples and wash of the water moved past them and gave the humps the appearance of movement.

The phenomenon would therefore be one of waves and water currents.

In 1957 Mrs Whyte published her book, in which she recorded statements from some eighty individual eyewitnesses, together with sketches and a number of photographs, showing what people claimed to be the Monster they had seen, swimming about undaunted in the loch!

4 The map and the Monster

Assuming for a moment there really is a Monster in Loch Ness and that reports about it being very large are true, a number of practical questions immediately spring to mind: how did it get in in the first place?—what does it feed on?—what is to stop it getting out if it wants to?—and why is it so infrequently seen? Questions like these are entirely relevant, and a sensible attempt must be made to answer each, but before doing so it would be as well to glance at a map and just see what sort of a place we are dealing with.

Any good Ordnance Survey map of one inch to the mile or better provides a clear idea of the topographical features around the loch, and, to some extent, within it. At very first sight it can be seen to be quite different to the usual run of lochs, which have inlets and bays and the irregular shore line associated with scenic motor rides, picnics and bathing parties. Loch Ness is absolutely straight, and along the major portion of its length its walls are of rock, precipitous both above and below the waterline. It is long and narrow and enormously deep, containing nearly three times as much water as Loch Lomond, the only other Scottish loch of comparable size. The actual volume of water contained has been calculated at some 263,000 million cubic feet; this huge mass of liquid acts like a hot-water bottle on the land immediately surrounding it, giving off, in winter, a vast amount of heat collected and stored within it during the summer months. It is in fact a 'heat sink', and affects the land around it in just the same way the Gulf Stream spreads its warming mass about the shores of the British Isles, fostering a temperate climate in spite of latitude comparable to that of northern Russia. Because of this effect the countryside about the loch, or that part of which is not precipitous, is green and pleasant. In winter snow rarely lies for more than a few hours, and the water never freezes: in fact its temperature varies little winter or summer. Water at approximately 42° Fahrenheit can be found at the bottom of the loch all year round, and although the surface temperature varies with the seasons to some extent, this difference is soon balanced out by convection currents and the general mixing of the various temperature and density levels.

The mean average depth for the whole area of the loch stands at about 430 ft, but the greater part of it goes down to 700 ft and more; the deepest part is off Urquhart Castle, more than twice the mean depth of the North Sea. The water is uncontaminated but it is stained a peaty colour and becomes opaque at a depth of only a few feet. At 50 ft or so divers have complained of a complete and very frightening blackness, and most are happy to return to the surface, such is the mystery of the place. It is this peat discoloration which gives the loch a curious inky appearance when viewed from surrounding hillsides, particularly noticeable when the surface is calm and cloud or mist obscures the sun, casting shadows.

Local tradition suggests that below water level, huge caves exist in the plunging rock walls forming the sides of the trench, in which the Monster is supposed to lurk, but it was not until sonar work in 1970 that evidence was found in support of this. Existing charts show depth levels from end to end of the loch, and a section taken about half-way down its length shows up to advantage the almost sheer side walls of rock and the flat bottom, suggesting a bed of several hundred feet of silt, brought down by the innumerable burns and the six main rivers discharging directly into the loch, which are together capable of producing sudden changes in water level. A rise of 24 inches has been recorded in a matter of only a few hours, but this astonishing variation is not difficult to understand when it is appreciated that a rainfall of only one quarter of an inch adds nearly 11 million tons of water to the catchment area draining into the loch, which has but one effective outlet: the river Ness at the north-eastern end, running out into the Moray Firth and the sea.

Seasonal changes in water level vary to some extent, depending on rainfall and evaporation, and a maximum variation of 7 ft 4 in. has been recorded by the Caledonian ship canal authorities, to whom it is a matter of concern. The canal itself cannot be considered an outlet from the loch: the amount of water needed to operate the locks is so small in relation to the normal discharge through the river Ness, it can almost be disregarded; but this is no measure of inactivity in the canal. Numbers of small ships and fishing vessels make use of this vital link each day.

Between the north-east end and the sea there are seven separate locks, and between Fort Augustus and Loch Linnhe there are no less than nineteen. The gates are kept closed, except when actually in use. It is out of the question to suspect that an animal the size of the Monster could slip through without attracting attention, even if this was physically possible, bearing in mind that lock gates are only opened and closed momentarily to allow the passage of a ship which itself occupies the greater part of each lock as it passes through it. Neither could the Monster be expected to squeeze through the small sluice openings nor avoid the watchful eyes of the canal employees who are instructed to report any unnatural disturbance seen, when working ships through the confines of the system. No such report has ever been recorded, of any consequence, and there can be no doubt at all that an animal 30–40 ft in length could never get in and out of the Loch through this canal system unobserved. Such being the case, the only alternative route lies in the river Ness, but here the situation is just as improbable.

The town of Inverness, a pleasant tidy place of some 30,000 people, straddles the river at the point where it flows out into the Beauly Firth. Although the river is 50 or 60 yards wide it is but a few feet deep, and to accept that any large animal could make its way upstream virtually through the centre of the town, un-noticed, is simply absurd. Even if it did so, seven or eight miles further upstream it would encounter Telford's weir, at the point where the river connects with Loch Dochfour, which presents an almost impassable obstacle.

All things considered, both the canal and river exits must be ruled out. Unless some alternative route can be found for the Monster there is little doubt it has been contained within the loch for a very long time; but before accepting this view entirely the question of a subterranean link with the sea should be considered.

It has been argued, somewhat naively perhaps, that passages of this sort could explain some of the more puzzling characteristics and problems posed by the Monster. The infrequency of sightings might be accounted for by a purely temporary population of Monsters which find their way into the loch on rare occasions to breed, and then return to the sea. In this case the matter of food supply would cease to present such a problem to the zoologists. But if the facts are considered sensibly there is, quite literally, no such easy way out. The surface of Loch Ness stands some 52 ft above mean sea level and any underwater connection with the sea would have to be of small dimensions or the loch level would gradually fall until the mouth of the passage became exposed;

but if it was of small size, unable to drain the inflow of water from rivers and burns, the current through it could be fairly rapid, dependent on the head of water at the point where it entered the loch, and it is difficult to imagine any large animal thrashing its way blindly through miles of underground passageways against a swirling torrent of water. No, the case for an underground link with the sea is quite insubstantial, and although it is wise not to overlook even remote possibilities, it seems the Monster can safely be accepted as a permanent resident without any means of escape; other than by an overland route, which is of course even more improbable.

Having now answered one question in the negative; the question 'can the Monster get out of the loch if it wants to?', we are faced with another more difficult question, 'how is it possible to explain the presence of the animal at all, and why should it be indigenous to this one particular loch in northern Scotland?' But before attempting to answer this it is necessary to proceed with a more detailed examination of the structure and topography of the place.

The Great Glen of Scotland stretches from the west coast to the east coast in an uninterrupted straight line, marking the course of a colossal crack or fault in the earth's surface, parts of which have now filled with water. Starting on the west coast with a sea loch, Loch Linnhe, it is possible to proceed up through the Caledonian Canal into freshwater lochs strung out in a line; from Lochy into Oich and then the Ness, and from there into the shallow salt waters of the Beauly Firth and Moray Firth and out into the North Sea, a journey of a hundred miles or so. The mountains that surround this area are of very ancient rock formation, dating back some 300 million years to the Caledonian period, and the Great Glen appears to be the product of a horizontal rift in which the northern part of the country has slipped sideways on the southern part. Although schools of thought vary to some extent on this issue, there is evidence to suggest the actual movement may have been as much as 60–70 miles. In most geological faults, rock displacement is in the vertical plane, but relieving movement depends on the direction in which the pressures act within the earth's crust, and it is possible for areas of rock to shear sideways *en masse*, along a splitline, in the manner sometimes displayed on a smaller scale in earthquakes, when gaping fissures appear and local movement of rock and soil becomes apparent. Whatever the original cause, the Great Glen demonstrates a type of rupture which is most uncommon, though not unique, in the earth's surface, and in its path a ditch has formed of quite unusual character. The original disturbance in this titanic balance of natural forces occurred millions of years ago, but local earth tremors indicate the area must still be a focal point for stresses and strains as yet unrelieved.

Looking at the area surrounding the loch as it stands today, it must appear very different to those ancient times. Gone are the towering mountains eroded away by the passage of countless centuries, by wind, and extremes of temperature, by the pulverizing effect of passing ice ages, leaving behind only the jagged remains of what once stood, now softened by soil and forests and the cultivated fields of man; and if we study the map and the contours and details on it, then follow the line of lakeshore road, it is possible to form in the mind a fair impression of the place and the features surrounding it.

Approaching the loch from the north-eastern end, taking General Wade's military road from Inverness leading to the southern shore, a first glimpse of the great loch is obtained from the downhill gradient two or three miles to the east of Dores, a small village nestling amongst trees on the very edge of the water. From Dores westwards the narrow single track runs parallel with the rocky shore and almost level with it, but the view is almost entirely obscured by a tangle of trees and undergrowth fencing off the water. Some few miles further on the road emerges and winds its way along the foreshore at the base of towering hillsides rising abruptly to peak at 1,400 ft in a series of knolls and craggy escarpments, overlooking the loch.

Here it is possible to see the water, although much of the view is still obscured by clumps of bushes and saplings. A little further on, the road, now almost down to water level, rounds an outcrop of rock, in a sudden blind curve, before ascending once more into trees. At this place so close to the water, a protecting stone wall stands like a parapet, from the top of which a magnificent view is obtained in all directions. To the right and left a vast expanse of water stretches as far as the eye can see, and in front, the opposite shore lies silent and remote. Slightly to the right Urquhart Bay can be seen in the distance, with the barely visible tumbled remains of a castle guarding the entrance to it.

Proceeding westwards again the village of Inverfarigaig appears, a few neat houses high up on the shore; then over a bridge the road ascends to a height of 300 ft and burrows deep into a stand of fir trees, completely hiding the loch for another mile or two,

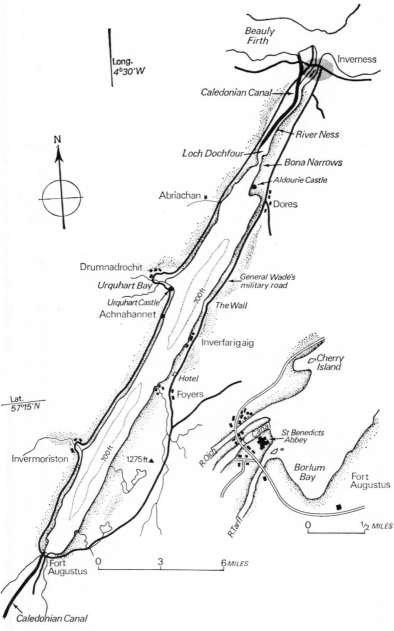

Figure 6 Loch Ness.

emerging suddenly high up on the hillside overlooking the village of Foyers. Here a river runs into the loch forming a promontory and crescent bay, with a shelving muddy beach, hiding for once the usual rocky shoreline. The land below looks flat in contrast to the mountain scenery surrounding it; strangely peaceful and dotted with steep gabled cottages.

Climbing even higher, the road slants away across the face of the hillside, and a view of the loch below develops in panoramic splendour. Of a sudden it seems we are looking down into a giant trench filled with ink, and yet across it the far shore seems close enough to touch; but on second glance tiny vehicles can be seen and heard scuttling along the distant terraced motor way: like coloured toys, providing the balance of perspective. Swinging away, the road breasts a hill then noses down a steep gradient shutting off the scenery behind it. From here to Fort Augustus, some 14 miles distant, the loch is seen no more, but in compensation, a magnificent jagged landscape spreads around us, with the ribbon of road undulating across it as far as the eye can see; following the track of the old garrison supply route of bygone days. Travelling on, climbing slowly, we reach the highest point of all, 1,275 ft above sea level, before starting the long descent down the twisting winding track, past Loch Tarff and Allt Doe burn, down towards Fort Augustus, laid out peacefully beneath at the south-western end of the loch, behind the sweep of Borlum Bay.

Fort Augustus is a small place, more than a village and yet less than a town, facing directly on to the most beautiful part of the loch perhaps, though this is a distinction difficult to make. Here, the Caledonian canal and the two rivers Oich and Tarff enter the loch, depositing mud and silt by slow degree, extending the flat fertile land on which the township stands today, and on the very edge overlooking the waters, the proud buildings of St Benedict's Abbey stand as if in quiet reflection, set about with trees and the greenery of lawns.

Passing through the place, the clustered shops and houses distract attention for a moment, and as we join the motor road leading along the northern shore towards Inverness, some 30 miles distant, the sense of expectancy and mystery is lost. No longer do we travel eager to peer around the next bend, awaiting new surprises, waterfalls and other scenic splendours; instead the well-constructed highway races on ahead, screened from the loch by a barrier of trees and bushes. From Fort Augustus to Invermoriston and then as far again to Urquhart Castle little can be seen of either shore, but to the right across the water a wall of scowling rock reaches high into the sky above, sparsely clad in mountain greenery, and it is this 10-mile stretch of uninhabited shoreline which seems to hold the greatest promise of scaly monsters. From above it is almost unapproachable, blocked off by 1,000 feet of near vertical cliff plunging down into the loch to a depth of 600 ft and more, and from below it can be reached only by boat; a remote and forbidding place, and yet strangely beautiful, standing through time in splendid, lofty isolation.

Journeying on, 16 miles or so to the eastwards, well past the bay at Foyers, the road momentarily clears the fence of obstructing trees and swings left, away from the loch to circuit Urquhart Bay, through the village of Drumnadrochit. At the point of the turn, several hundred feet above the water a panoramic view develops across the wide eastern reaches of the loch, and below, at Strone point, the famous Castle Urquhart stands, its ancient ruins the playground of children and tourists, a silent monument to a warlike past.

Beyond Urquhart Bay, the road runs on high up on the hillside which climbs another thousand feet or so above it, but here there are no trees and a bird's eye view is gained across the water. From a point some two miles eastwards, the bottom of the loch slowly begins to shelve upwards, until, off Tor point, the depth stands at no more than 300 ft. This is the only part of the loch where gradual shelving occurs with a gradient of no more than a hundred feet per mile, indicating the presence of glacial deposits; remains from the last ice age when the whole area was sheathed in ice several thousand feet thick in places. Here the loch narrows suddenly, and as we travel the remaining mile or two past Aldourie Castle on the opposite shore, the road descends again almost to water level and the loch takes on a more peaceful and mundane air with boats and yachts bobbing about at anchor, and as the distant shingle beach at Lochend draws closer depth of water decreases; 200, 100 and then only 50 ft separate the surface from the bottom until both meet together in a wash of ripples on this stretch of eastern shore; with a shallow overflow of water draining out through the Bona narrows into Loch Dochfour below.

This is the end of our picturesque lochside journey, in the course of which an astonishing variety of colour and scenery has met the eye, creating a lasting impression—of contrasts and grandeur, of sombre shadows and sparkling light and the many tricks of wind upon the water. This is Loch Ness, and in our journey around it we have obtained an impression of scale, which is most important. The enormous size and depth of the loch stagger the imagination; from one end to the other it is deeper than the sea surrounding the British Isles, as far out as the edge of the continental shelf, and it is large enough to make a home for half a dozen Monsters—the Monster *could* be real in terms of scale, of that there is no longer any doubt at all; but if this is so, on what does it feed and from where is the food supply replenished ?

Such great and powerful creatures could be expected to eat an enormous amount of something, be it fish or weed or plankton in the water, without an abundant supply of which none could survive for very long. There is little evidence of weed at any level, but a reddish brown algae adheres to stones along the rocky shoreline and recent plankton samples suggest that at certain seasons microscopic organisms abound within these waters. When we turn to the more likely source of supply, fish, the situation is very different. The loch contains a healthy stock of salmon and fish of up to 30 lb or more are caught each year, fresh run from the sea. Trout are also to be had in numbers and grow to a very unusual size, 15–20 lb, which must be a near record for brown trout in British waters. To local people these fish are known as 'black' trout, due to the marked discoloration resulting from a life spent in peaty water, and they bear little outward resemblance to their more ornamental cousins swimming in freshwater streams. A few pike are found at the mouths of rivers and recent echo soundings suggest the presence of schools of char swimming at very considerable depths; but amongst this fishy population the eel occupies perhaps the most important and unexpected place.

Not so many years ago, when eels were more in demand as an item of popular human diet, professional Irish fishermen would come to the loch and sink their lines parallel to the shore, with hundreds of baited hooks; and men who have watched these operations speak of astonishing catches suggesting an overall population of millions of eels throughout the loch. More recently this belief is borne out by the views of an expert ichthyologist, who is of the opinion that the loch acts as a sort of vast eel trap in which migrating eels make a home instead of returning to the sea to breed in normal fashion. Certainly some very large eels have been caught from time to time, and this suggests the presence of an adult population of very long standing. Eels are cannibalistic, and every year uncounted millions of young elvers swim up British rivers and those that enter the loch may well replenish the larder for their larger brethren already in residence, which in turn become a meal for the Monster. It is an interesting theory, the proof of which may well solve the most difficult problem of all connected with the Monster; adding yet another unique feature to the natual history of the place, and the story of the loch about which the mists of improbability are beginning to lift a little.

Reassessing the facts for a moment, with due regard for probabilities, it seems that Loch Ness is a place big enough for Monsters to live in, and with a potential and perhaps inexhaustible food supply—should these creatures choose to live on a diet of fish. This is an encouraging start, and a base for future investigations, but there are still a number of vital questions as yet unanswered. What are these animals? Have they always lived in the loch? Are they related to any other known species? And if they are, what are these other species, and where do they live?—and so on. Questions like these are inevitable, and have been asked many times before, but if it is not yet possible to provide answers which are known to be correct there is no good reason why they should simply be disregarded—on the contrary it is essential to try and get to the bottom of the mystery by process of *active* research and constructive thinking. Every clue must be examined, and nothing must be discarded until we are sure it has no value or significance. So much evidence has in the past been pompously ignored or brushed aside simply because it does not fit the pattern of conventional thinking, it is little wonder the Monster continues to live in an atmosphere of myth and doubt and almost hopeless misunderstanding.

This is a trap that must be avoided, because very little connected with the Monster appears to have much to do with conventional thinking—but from among these remaining questions there is only one that needs to be considered within the scope of this chapter; which has to do with mountains and maps—and that is, 'have the Monsters always lived in the Loch?'

To this question there can of course be no cut and dried reply, but if the facts about the loch and its formation are considered, going right back into its geological history, the answer is certainly 'no', for a number of very good reasons.

About 10,000 years ago, at the end of the last ice age, the levels of the ocean began to rise as the ice slowly melted flooding many of the glacial valleys gouged out beneath; of which the fjords of Norway and the sea lochs of Scotland are fine examples. At first the water rose about 200 ft. Later as the great weight of ice became less, the crust of the earth, which itself floats on a mass of molten rock, readjusted itself, and in places the land began to rise also. For a period of time, about 5,000 years ago, both the water and land rose at the same rate and clearly defined beaches were formed around the sea-coasts; then about 2,000 years later, the water stopped rising, but the land slowly continued. In certain places this process is still going on, though of course at an imperceptible rate. Scotland and Norway are thought to be lifting slowly in this manner today, and in these countries proof of this interesting sequence of events can be found in the form of raised beaches around the sea-coasts and is particularly noticeable in north-western Norway. Raised beaches at different levels can also be found, corresponding to the synchronous rise of land and water which varied from place to place.

The most famous beaches of this form are known as the '50 ft beaches'; that is 50 ft above present sea-level, marking the level of the sea some 3,000–4,000 years ago. Originally, the whole of the Great Glen must have been submerged by the sea, but as the land rose, Loch Ness would have become a separate arm of the sea, remaining so for a very long time: and this is a most important fact. During this time creatures of the sea must have swum in and out of it, enjoying perhaps the advantage of good fishing and a temporary freedom from deep-sea predators. It may be that as time went by some found that within the protecting walls of rock the waters possessed all that life required, and as the land gradually rose, reducing accessibility to the sea, they would have become less and less inclined to leave the place. Eventually, a sand bar would form at the seaward end, tidal at first, but collecting more and more silt, forming in time a plug through which a river would begin to cut a path spilling off the water from the loch behind it; depositing more silt in passage; building the dam which shut off the loch from the sea, holding its waters in check at the original sea-level, now lifted by the rise in land to a height of 52 ft *above* the present sea level—as the map so clearly states.

5 The surgeon's photograph

In February 1960 work on the analysis was almost complete. Towards the end, I had begun to find it tedious sorting through such a great number of reports, many of which were repetitive and contained only a few phrases of useful detail. I welcomed the prospect of action at the lochside, or for that matter any opportunity to study the Monster from a different angle or approach.

One evening, glancing through the book *More than a Legend* with which I was by now thoroughly familiar, my eye came to rest on the most famous photograph of all—the surgeon's picture of the head and neck. For months past this picture had fascinated me and I had peered at it on many occasions—wondering, like so many others before me, whether or not it was a fake. As a photographer I could see much that suggested it was not, from a purely technical point of view, but the picture it portrayed was so extraordinary, I found myself searching for some simple explanation—could it be a branch perhaps, sticking up out of the water? or a model of some kind? or an elephant's trunk? or some other ordinary object creating an illusion? I turned the picture this way and that, trying to find the solution, peering at it from every angle, eyes half closed in concentration, trying to find some telltale scrap of hidden detail—and then I held it at arm's length, hoping to gain a better sense of perspective; and in doing this my eye caught sight of something I had never noticed before, which immediately sprang into focus and relationship with the other parts of the picture surrounding it. For a moment it had no meaning, though now I could see it clearly, and then its true significance dawned upon me and I realized, for the first time, with complete assurance, the picture was *not* a fake and that the Loch Ness Monster was real and tangible; a living animal—or one that had been real and alive when the picture was taken in 1934.

I put the book down, knowing that there could be no mistake about it—the picture showed the head and neck of an animal unknown to science; and that from this moment of acceptance, my search for it would begin in deadly earnest!

The detail in the picture was obscure, so difficult to see in fact I must have peered at it at least a dozen times before noticing anything unusual, and then only because I had held the photo away from me at arm's length.

Had these marks been introduced deliberately as part of a fake, then the fake was pointless, because they were so faint the great majority of people would never see them, and the few who did would not appreciate their meaning unless they were thoroughly familiar with reports about the Monster. This alone was sufficiently convincing, but there was more to it than that—the obscure marks had a *secondary* meaning—and proved a point which had nothing to do with the Monster directly. It concerned a fundamental physical law with which, as an engineer, I was familiar. Had I not been in this category of persons I could not have known what this point, or the secondary meaning was. Altogether, the subtleties involved in the picture proved beyond doubt it was genuine.

Encouraged by this unexpected and exciting discovery, I decided to go on looking in the hope of finding more hidden detail, and it was not long before my efforts were rewarded. There were three other significant features in the picture which had previously escaped attention. Finally, when I could find nothing more, I decided to marshal all the facts in the form of a brief report, and try to use this to persuade others the picture was really genuine—and therefore of enormous scientific interest. In due course I did this, and on 20th February 1960 part of this report appeared within the covers of the *London Illustrated News*; but for the purpose of showing the reader what it was I saw in the photograph, a shortened version is now appended, together with a sketch pointing out the various features of interest and significance.

Report on a photograph—

1   *Subject*
A critical examination of the photograph obtained in April of 1934 by a London surgeon, reputedly showing the head and neck of the Loch Ness Monster.

2.   *The recorded facts*
According to the statements recorded in Mrs Whyte's book, the following essential facts apply:

(a) The man who obtained the picture was a member of the medical profession.

(b) The photo was obtained by chance, at an early hour in the morning, with a quarter-plate camera and telephoto lens, at a range of two or three hundred yards.

(c) The four plates were developed immediately afterwards by a reputable chemist in Inverness—a Mr George Morrison.

(d) The best picture resulting was subsequently published in the *Daily Mail*, but the photographer preferred to avoid publicity in connection with it.

3. *Analysis*

(a) *The recorded facts:* these seem to be honest and uncomplicated and therefore hardly the work of a hoaxer or publicity seeker.

The fact the picture was obtained by chance and in the early morning fits the pattern of usual sightings.

If the account of how the picture was obtained was untrue, and the picture deliberately faked, it is unlikely the photographer would have had the plates developed independently by a chemist in Inverness.

(b) *Faking:* as any photographer knows, really good faking is extremely difficult without careful preparation and the right facilities and equipment.

Generally speaking it can be done either by touching up the film negative or by creating a false impression as to scale and subject matter by using, or superimposing, models and background material. The trouble with these techniques is that the film negative always gives the show away if it has been tampered with, and the use of models almost invariably produces some detectable error with regard to scale, perspective, proportion or appearance.

In this case, so long after the event, there is no ready means of checking on the original negative, but there is nothing in the original account of how the picture was obtained to suggest faking; in fact the opposite is true. The straightforward testimony is quite believable and there seems little reason to suspect the photographer or the man who developed the plates of interfering with them; and with regard to the second faking technique, there is nothing in the picture that is obviously out of proportion or perspective and although the object seen is unnatural in the true sense of the word, it appears in a natural pose which is both graceful and curiously attentive; as though the creature is on the alert for something.

These facts suggest that the picture is not faked, or alternatively that if it is, it has been treated with great cleverness.

(c) *Quality:* the account states the picture was obtained with a quarter-plate camera and telephoto lens, and although the focal length of this lens is not stated, it is possible to generalize fairly by saying that such a combination could be expected to produce a relatively large photographic image at a considerable range, and thus lessen the need to enlarge when making prints.

Due to the year, 1934, it is almost certain that a relatively slow orthochromatic fine grain emulsion would have been used, producing the good tone graduation common to this type of film, or in this case, plate. The print, though somewhat contrasty, is of fair quality and there is little evident graininess, which indicates that if it was enlarged it was probably not enlarged very much.

(d) *Content:* at first glance, the picture does not seem to be filled with detail—there appears to be the head and neck of some strange animal sticking up out of the water in silhouette, casting its shadow on the water, and on either side where the neck joins the (presumed) body, there is evidence of something solid breaking the surface.

The water itself looks ordinary enough, with two kinds of ripples apparent on it—lines of parallel wind-blown ripples moving through the picture, and concentric rings of ripples emanating from the central disturbance, the neck.

(e) *Significant detail:* upon really close examination, there are certain rather obscure features in the picture which have a profound significance. As these relate separately to the object seen, the head and neck, and also to the water surface, it is best to consider them independently under these two headings.

With regard to the head and neck, the following descriptive phrases recorded by different people are worth consideration—

> It had a face like a goat, with two stumps on top of its head, like sheeps' horns broken off—It was like a huge swan on the water, with only part of the body showing—The head and neck were raised like a bird on the water—The neck thickened suddenly to join the first hump.

It would be difficult more aptly to describe the profile in the photo, and yet the people who made these comments were describing the Monster they had seen themselves, and *not* the shape in the photo—which *does* have a face a bit like that of a goat; on top of which can just be seen a tiny knob or protrusion—and which *does* exhibit a sudden conical thickening of the neck at a point where it appears to join the submerged body—but considering the picture again there is more to be seen. To the right of the neck, just breaking the surface, there appears to be a solid object, and well to the left and behind the neck, there is another mark of some sort. Could these be parts of the forward flippers, which people have claimed to have seen? It is not possible to tell—but that is just the point! Had these marks been deliberately introduced as part of a fake, they would be without purpose, because they are too indefinite, and yet to students of the evidence they may conceivably mean something; but there are very few people in this category. It seems therefore that these marks are either part of a very subtle fake, or genuinely part of the Monster.

(*f*) *The water surface:* looking at the picture held at arm's length, there are two kinds of visible ripples on the surface: the parallel lines of wind-blown ripples, coursing along under the influence of a breeze, and a large concentric ring of ripples caused by the central disturbance, the neck. At first glance, this is all that can be seen, but looking again it is possible to make out a second smaller ring of ripples, caused by some disturbance well to the rear of the neck.

This second ring is very important. Being smaller in diameter than the ring caused by the neck, it follows that it must have been generated *after* the head and neck broke surface in the position shown, because in water, all ripples, whether caused by a big splash or a minute disturbance, move outwards *at the same speed*—it is only the height or 'amplitude' of the ripple that varies. This is fundamental, and means that ripples cannot catch up on each other; and this proves irrefutably that with the neck appearing in the position shown, there is also a part of the animal underwater, considerably behind it.

These facts suggest that the picture is not a fake.

At about this time I enjoyed another welcome boost to morale. I had written to the proprietors of the small hotel at Foyers, half way along the southern shore of the loch, booking a room, and asking if there had been any recent signs of the Monster—never thinking for a moment my remarks would be taken seriously. In the polite letter I received in reply, the following statement appeared:

1   Small ring of ripples

2   Opposing arcs

3   Larger ring of ripples

4   Parallel wind-blown ripples

5   Ring of ripples arch over straight wind-blown wavelet

i.e.

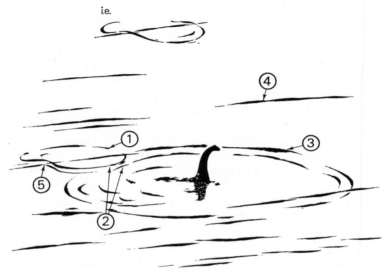

Figure 7   Points to look for on the water surface in the surgeon's photograph.

according to substantiated reports, Nessie was seen a
number of times last spring, and early in the summer and a
few times in the autumn—but as far as we know, there have
been no more recent sightings. A motor-coach party had a
good view of her in mid-July, from the road leading from
the hotel to the village of Foyers . . .

Reading this matter-of-fact account, I realized that unless I was
being deliberately misled, there could be little doubt the Monster
was still alive and kicking; a creature of flesh and blood *living in
the present*. It is difficult to describe the effect this had upon me—
for over a year I had been working in a purely academic atmosphere of study and interest, remote from the loch and reality and
during this time I had come to believe in the Monster because of
the work I had done on paper, checking and rechecking what others
had said about it; and as a result I had come to think in terms of

a paper Monster, a beast made up of certain statistical lengths and percentage probabilities, lacking the movement, colour and breadth, which are together the essence of reality—but now it seemed to have suddenly come to life: to have assumed these vital earthly qualities!

6 Monster hunt

On 16 April 1960 I set out from my home in Reading in a small car loaded to the roof with equipment. I knew that the months of work and planning lay behind, and that if I did not find the Monster I could at least fulfil a number of other useful tasks at the loch; which would add to my general fund of knowledge and perhaps prepare the way for future expeditions.

I was on my own, because in spite of making every effort to persuade others to come along, both friends and relatives alike had declined the invitation! Business matters, and the chilly prospect of days of fruitless searching, spent out of doors in the rain, perhaps, had brought a rush of polite refusals; but I was not perturbed, and the prospect of attempting to search the 14,000 acres of water unaided was very much a challenge.

During the planned five-day stay at the loch I had to accomplish three things: look for the Monster, each day, from dawn till dusk; carry out a physical reconnaissance, and map those parts of the loch which were best for camera sites and camping places; and in the evenings, talk to local people who claimed to have seen the creature. This would make a very long day and if I hoped to be successful, I would have to maintain mobility and a state of instant readiness, regardless of wind, or rain, or bodily fatigue. It would require a determined effort, and yet it was not without promise of reward. From end to end the loch was relatively narrow and with the telephoto lens I had on loan, I could reach out and film the Monster up to a range of a mile or more—if only I could see it.

Driving up through the industrial heart of England I joined the Great North Road, and late that evening drove through the gates of a Northumberland farm, glad to have completed the first leg of the wearisome journey. The following day I took the route up through Edinburgh, across the Firth of Forth by Queen's ferry, under the magnificent soaring spans of the old railway bridge, and soon into the mountains and glens to the north.

Looking about, as any stranger would, I began to wonder whether I had made a mistake coming so early in the year. Inside the car it was deceptively warm and pleasant, but when I opened the window a freezing wind swirled about, bringing with it a taste of the rigours to come.

There was little traffic on the road which wound its lonely way ahead, far into the distance. My spirits began to sink and for the first time in months I was plagued again with doubt. Was it all a fairy tale after all? could there really be a Monster in the loch? what on earth was I doing driving on all alone, into this land of rock and ice? Perhaps it *was* all a lot of rubbish—the misguided chatter of silly people! But it was too late to turn back. For the hundredth time I added up the facts and arrived at the same encouraging total, and as I neared the journey's end I left behind the bleak and sullen mountain scenery and in place of it a softer more hospitable landscape appeared—the seaward end of the Great Glen of Scotland, the huge rift dividing north and south, linking the west and eastern seaboard.

I drove into Inverness, a mellow tidy place, with shops and banks and all the outward signs of life of a modern thriving township, so different from the outpost I had imagined—and then out along the little road running parallel with the shallow river Ness, on towards the loch itself. I had several miles to go, and the light was beginning to fail, so before reaching the water I stopped the car and set up my camera equipment, determined that whatever happened the Monster would never catch me unawares.

I had three cameras with me, a tripod mounted 16-mm Bolex ciné with 135-mm telephoto lens loaded with black and white film; an 8-mm Kodak ciné, and a good German 35-mm both loaded with colour film. The smaller cameras were for stand by purposes only, and would be used if I ran out of 16-mm film, or had time to spare.

I had removed the left-hand front seat from inside the car, and a folding canoe lay in its place, and on top of that a load of other equipment. My tactics were simple enough—I would use the car as a mobile platform, and chase the Monster, should I see it in the distance, and thus try to close the range and obtain those vital close-up pictures. I knew the animal was supposed to be enormous, and that if it surfaced it might splash about for ten or twenty minutes. With my binoculars, I could scan the loch for two or three miles at least in either direction; with the car I could quickly close the gap—and if the Monster was then still too far away I could, in theory, launch the assembled canoe from the roof of the car and paddle off towards it! This was the temporary plan I had decided on, but I knew that it would need to be flexible, adjusted in whatever way seemed best in the light of experience gained on the shores of the loch.

Driving down the narrow road leading to the southern shore,

I got a first glimpse of the loch from a point on high ground about a mile from its eastern extremity. Breasting a rise, I stopped—and there, stretching away into the distance as far as the eye could see lay a great shining pool of water, reflecting the last rays of a wintry sun, framed on either side by blackened walls of mountains. I stood for a moment gazing down at the scene, much affected by the strange beauty of the place; and then, as the light was fading, turned and climbed back into the car, conscious for the first time of being tired. In the last two days I had spent nearly twenty-five hours cramped in the driver's seat, and that was more than enough.

I drove on to the village of Dores, in amongst the trees, and then out along General Wade's military road, the narrow single track running parallel to the southern shore, almost level with the water. As I drove along I instinctively craned my neck, staring out over the water, hoping vainly to see the Monster, but knowing all the while that I would not.

The road started to climb a little and the trees grew thicker—and then, several hundred yards ahead I saw a man at the roadside, peering out across the loch, pointing, and beyond him a woman and two children waving their arms in excitement.

Intrigued, I drove up closer, trying to drive and look all at once—and then, incredibly, two or three hundred yards from shore, I saw two sinuous grey humps breaking the surface with seven or eight feet of clear water showing between each. I looked again, blinking my eyes—but there it remained as large as life, lolling on the surface!

I swung the car across the road and locked the wheels, pulling up in a shower of gravel; and flinging open the doors, lifted the Bolex out, with its long ungainly tripod. I struggled to set it up on the uneven ground, and with palsied hands set about the task of getting the camera into action. I kept glancing at the loch, expecting to see the humps disappear in a sudden swirl of foam.

I knew the seconds must be flying by, but the unfamiliar camera—a mass of knobs and levers, glinting back at me in defiance—would not be hurried. By now my hands were shaking to such an extent I could do little useful with them; but when at last, almost in despair, I squinted through the sight ready to film, the humps were still in place, calmly awaiting events: floating on the surface, strangely docile and inanimate.

For a moment I hesitated, my finger on the button, and then upon a sudden impulse reached for my binoculars in the car, and focused them upon it. Expanded seven times, the humps looked more impressive, larger than life it seemed, and yet when I examined them carefully it was just possible to see a single hairlike twig sprouting out of the one to the right—with a solitary leaf upon it, fluttering gaily in the breeze.

Slowly and deliberately I put the equipment back in the car, feeling rather foolish, and drove off up the road: watched by curious eyes of the man ahead. It was probably a good thing the Monster had turned out to be a floating tree-trunk. To have filmed it too soon would have almost been a disappointment— and my first attempt to get into action quickly had not deserved success. I had made a hopeless mess of it, wasting time fiddling about in a state of wild confusion, and I realized that if I was ever to film successfully, I would need to drill myself in the use of the camera as though my life depended on it, practising every moment until reactions came with instinctive speed and complete calmness.

By now the light was fading fast, so I drove on to the little hotel at Foyers perched high up on the hillside commanding a splendid view of the loch. Hugh Rowand, the English proprietor, came out to greet me, and leading the way showed me to my room upstairs, overlooking the water, two or three hundred feet below. He seemed a very pleasant person and politely ignored the tell-tale cameras in the car, and I was glad that he did; a little sheepish still from my encounter with the tree-trunk!

I washed and changed, and ate dinner; but before going to bed I set up the tripod and camera and worked on my drill until I was proficient. To operate a 16-mm ciné camera of the type I had with me required five separate deliberate adjustments, each of importance, and two more on the tripod. I knew that to omit any one of these or to make a mistake about them might well result in a defective film—or worse, an opportunity missed for ever.

When everything was up to standard, I went to bed, having first set the alarm to go off at 4.30 the following morning— half an hour before the dawn.

The hunt begins in earnest

Daily Log, April 18th, 1960. Easter Monday

4.30 a.m.	Got up.
5 a.m.—9.30 a.m.	Drove round the loch.
9.30 a.m.—6.30 p.m.	Survey work. Area 1 (see map).
7 p.m.—9 p.m.	Foyers Point.

RESULTS: Monster—nil: Survey—useful: Interviews—one good: Total watching time, approx. 16 hours.

Behind these cryptic remarks in my daily log lay a varied and rewarding day's activities, made after a rather discouraging start. At 3 a.m., only an hour or two after going to sleep, I had woken again, and as the hours ticked off into the morning I lay in miserable suspense, waiting for the alarm to ring.

Outside, the loch lay cold and dim, far below and out of reach in the very early light. A few minutes before sunrise I drove off up the steeply climbing road to Fort Augustus, 14 miles to the west. Twisting and turning out of sight of the loch the tiny road climbed off into the mountains, and I followed it in a state of complete depression—and yet as the road climbed higher and higher, I could not help but look about in curiosity; and it was then that I became aware of different colour tones, and a gradual change in light. I stopped the car and got out to obtain a better view, and there to the east I saw a sight of quite extraordinary beauty—a great fiery ball of sun had arisen, and all about the jagged snow-capped peaks of mountains reflected its brilliant orange light! I stood for a moment entranced, gazing down at this wild and lovely scenery, feeling as though I had wandered into a dream. The air was fresh, and I began to realize that for all my doubts and chills there would be compensations in this lonely search for the Monster; which as yet had hardly begun. In the next five days I must inevitably spend time out of doors in country such as this, living and moving amongst the peaks, breathing this pure and fragrant mountain air.

Much encouraged I carried on to Fort Augustus, past the little Loch Tarff, glinting at the roadside, and then down the mountainside towards Loch Ness. I first caught sight of it again from a place 700 or 800 ft above the water, and realized what an ideal point of vantage it was. Below the western end of the loch could be clearly scanned, including the beach at Borlum Bay—the place where the Monster had been seen partly out of the water in 1934; but as the purpose of the journey was one of strict reconnaissance, I did not stop for long. I drove through the slumbering township, then back along the motor road along the northern shore, heading for Inverness. There were many miles to go and trees obscured the view, so I drove quickly and it was not until reaching Urquhart Bay 15 miles to the eastward that I gained an uninterrupted view of the water;

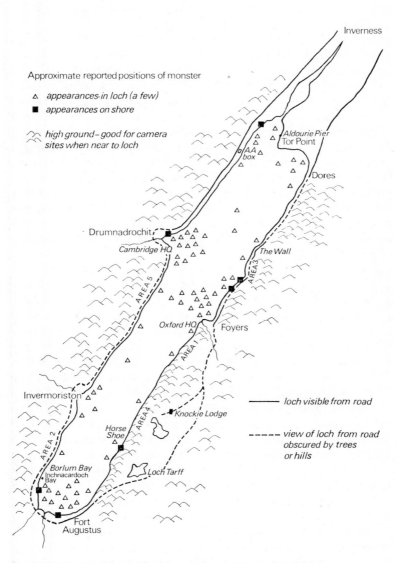

Figure 8   Map (not to scale) showing the positions of sightings.

but here the road ran so high up on the mountain-side and the loch below was so very great in width, I knew it must be outside the range of my telephoto lens.

I drove into Inverness, and then back along the southern shore to Foyers, arriving just in time for breakfast. I ate a welcome meal of bacon and eggs, and felt much the better for it. The trip around the loch, 70 miles or so, though a waste of time in looking for the Monster, had taught me several lessons. In the first place in order to keep within camera range I would need to concentrate the search to the western half of the loch. Secondly, the canoe did not appear to offer any real advantage and might therefore be discarded. Thirdly, due to the heavy growth of trees barring the view from two-thirds of the roads surrounding the loch it would be better to look for camera sites either at water level or above it on the hillside. As the latter seemed a more favourable proposition I set off to explore the hills to the west of the village of Foyers; driving the car as far as I could take it, then setting out on foot carrying my equipment.

I climbed to a point 1,000 feet above the water and then looking round decided to go no higher. To right and left as far as the eye could see the great loch stretched in panoramic splendour, and I realized at once that this was the ideal situation. With a really long-focus lens it would be possible to reduce the odds enormously from such a place—but without one, the extra height was merely a disadvantage. The lens I possessed was not of particular power, so I clambered down again to a lower level and spent the day sitting on a mossy ledge gazing down at the world around me, very much at ease. The sun shone, bringing with it warmth and colour, and a moving patchwork of light and shade on the surrounding hills and mountains, and as the day wore on I became attuned to the peaceful scene. Although there was no visible sign or disturbance in the still waters beneath, I felt the day had not been wasted, and returned to the hotel, sunburnt and cheerful.

After supper, standing on the patch of lawn outside the hotel, periodically scanning the loch with binoculars, I talked to the proprietor about the Monster. By now it was obvious what my intentions were and I had no desire or reason to conceal them. He had not been at the hotel for very long, but told me, with obvious sincerity, of a curious experience which he and his wife and two friends had had the previous spring, when watching the loch from the lawn on which we were now standing. Off the river mouth at Foyers, 600–700 yards distant, a large triangular object had appeared, sticking several feet out of the water; and this had suddenly shot off at incredible speed, travelling several hundred yards before submerging!

Mr Rowand wisely preferred not to make any predictions as to what the object might have actually been, but did admit quite freely that it was very extraordinary and that the speed at which it moved reminded him of a naval torpedo, streaking through the water.

Later, I was to find out that he had at one time been an aeronautical engineer like myself, and the manner in which he told the story was fittingly reserved and specific, and yet carried conviction with it. I was at once conscious of the truly great difference between the words of a written account, and those of an actual witness.

I enquired whether he knew of any other witnesses with whom I might talk, and was told that Hugh Gray still lived in Foyers village, down below—the man who had first photographed the Monster in 1934.

I drove off down hill at once, and found his cottage without difficulty but as Mr Gray was out, arranged to call again the following evening. There were several hours of daylight left, and I spent these on Foyers Point, gradually increasing lens apertures as the light slowly diminished until I knew it would no longer be possible to film the Monster even if I saw it—and so ended the first day of the hunt. A day starting with near defeat, but ending in encouragement.

Second day

Daily log April 19th, 1960

4.45 a.m.	Got up.
5.20 a.m.–9.10 a.m.	Watched Borlum Bay—patrolled area 2.
9.30 a.m.–4.30 p.m.	Watched Foyers Bay.
4.30 p.m.–5.15 p.m.	Interview with Mr Gray.
7.30 p.m.–9.30 p.m.	Surveyed and watched from area 3

RESULTS: Monster—nil: Survey—limited work: Interviews— one good: Total watching time, 15.05 hours.

By now I had become thoroughly engrossed with the hunt; and once again I set off for Fort Augustus at dawn, and spent an hour or two watching Borlum Bay, perched high up on the mountainside.

The scene below was completely peaceful—the loch like a sheet of polished glass; and I stayed in position until the first sounds of life could be heard. The sudden bark of a dog, the clatter of milk bottles, and then a distant shout—faint sounds, reaching up to my lofty perch, breaking the spell.

I coasted down the hill, and then patrolled the shore out towards Invermoriston, watching from various selected places. Away from the road, and through the protecting screen of trees, the far shore could be clearly seen and I searched every inch of it with binoculars, every rock and boulder, but without result—and then it began to rain. I retreated inside the car, and set up the camera on a shortened tripod in the place where the left-hand seat had been—an excellent arrangement, by which I could maintain the watch in any kind of weather. The telephoto lens peered out through the window, and by turning quickly in my seat I could bring the camera into action in a matter of seconds only.

Returning for breakfast, I continued to watch for the rest of the day in the manner recorded in the log, and at 4.30 p.m. as arranged I met Mr Gray in Foyers village. He proved to be a most courteous individual, and walked with me for a half a mile along the shore of the loch, to the exact spot where he claimed to have seen the Monster. He described his experience candidly, speaking with conviction; his account fitted the facts recorded by Mrs Whyte, in every detail. Walking back to the village, he told me he had seen the wake the Monster made on several occasions, and described in graphic terms the extraordinary bow wave building up, rushing down the loch at remarkable speed, *without anything visible* making it. Back at his cottage he showed me a print from the original film he had taken, and although it was of a poor quality it was possible to make out a sinuous shape in the water, and the ripples surrounding it, giving a fair impression of scale. I thanked Mr Gray for the time and trouble he had taken, and drove off to continue the watch.

It was clear enough that people who had actually *seen* the Monster, or what they presumed to be the Monster, had no doubts about hallucination, or being otherwise mistaken or misled. Because of this important fact I decided to try to talk to other witnesses—particular witnesses, people who by virtue of their work or profession were qualified to speak about the loch with assurance or authority. Alex Campbell, the water bailiff, for example, the man whose account I had first read in the magazine article—and the monks at St Benedict's Abbey, facing directly on to the water. I knew I would get the truth from them. It would clearly be worthwhile sacrificing a few hours of watching time if I could talk to other witnesses as assured as Mr Gray.

Well satisfied with the way things were going, I spent the rest of the day watching the loch from the mountainous terrain opposite Urquhart Castle—but without seeing any sign or monstrous disturbance.

Third day

Daily log Wednesday, April 20th.

5.00 a.m.	Got up, disgruntled.
5.20 a.m.– 9.10 a.m.	Watched Borlum Bay, and from area 2.
9.30 a.m.–10.30 a.m.	Watched Foyers Bay.
10.30 a.m.–12.30 p.m.	Watched from 'the Wall'.
12.30 p.m.– 2.30 p.m.	Visited Mrs Constance Whyte.
2.30 p.m.– 6.00 p.m.	Watched from various places; northern shore.
6.30 p.m.– 8.00 p.m.	Watched Foyers Bay (good news).
8.30 p.m.–10.15 p.m.	Visited Fort Augustus. Talked to Father A. J. Carruth at St Benedict's Abbey.

RESULTS: Monster—possibility of V wake: Survey—continued: Interviews—1 possible eyewitness, 2 non-witnesses: Total watching time, 10.50 hours.

I awoke with the alarm and journeyed to Fort Augustus, repeating the previous day's dawn activities. At the hotel the previous evening I had heard a curious rumour—a story circulating around the loch about a man who claimed to have seen the Monster partly out of the water on the shore, near a place called the 'horse-shoe'—a patch of scree, marking a precipitous slope on the inaccessible southern shore. The event was reported to have taken place seven or eight weeks previously, in February, and the man was said to have watched the creature for several minutes through binoculars!

There seemed to be no means of checking the story, but I was determined to try to find out what truth there might be in it, and that morning I sat for several hours opposite the 'horse-shoe' mark, peering through binoculars. The far shore at this point stood a little over a mile distant, but with a good pair of glasses it was quite possible to pick out boulders and rocks of only a foot or so in diameter—and I realized that if the man really had seen the Monster out of the water, and if it was only half as big as people generally reported, it must have been very clearly visible.

I sat, hopefully, amongst the rocks, with the early morning mist shrouding the mountain tops and the loch as smooth as a looking glass reflecting every detail of the trees and cliffs surrounding it. I sat without moving, conscious of the strange perfection of the place and the almost uncanny stillness—and then, a sudden explosion shook the ground around me. A tremendous *thunderclap* of noise, which echoed back and forth between the walls of rock, in rolling peals of thunder; grumbling and muttering, far off into the distance.

Intrigued by this curious incident, so early in the morning, two things struck me most forcibly about it. Without doubt, this was 'the din of blasting' which was said to have frightened the Monsters and brought them to the surface in the early 1930s with such remarkable frequency. Having now experienced the stunning effect of an explosion within the confines of this rocky place, and the echoes that followed on, I could well imagine there might be something in the theory. The shock must have been felt underwater for miles, and I wondered whether repeated charges such as these might be used in a deliberate future experiment—an attempt to bring the Monster to the surface, without any risk of harming it. The idea was certainly worth consideration, but while I pondered on it another thought occurred to me. If the Monster was still alive, and not an hallucination, the final proof of its existence, of its shape and form, would come as another explosion—the news of which would rumble round the world, and echo into history!

I returned to Foyers for breakfast, and later on that day drove through Inverness to the village of Clachnaharry, there to meet Mrs Constance Whyte, the author of the book. I had phoned her the day before and had arranged to discuss the Monster, a subject about which she obviously knew a very great deal. We sat and talked for an hour or two, engrossed in conversation, the focal point of which was of such great interest to both of us, and in this we enjoyed a mutual understanding, the foundation of a friendship which was to prove of great assistance in my future work at the loch. I learned the names of several outstanding witnesses, people who claimed to have seen the animal clearly, in some cases at a distance of only a few yards; in addition I found out much that concerned the history of the place, and of the many unsuccessful private attempts to solve the mystery. I would have liked to extend the visit but I had to get back to the loch; I took my leave knowing that we would later meet again.

One thing I had learned in particular from talking to Mrs Whyte—her book was the product of years of research, and although she had never seen the Monster herself, she had met and talked to a hundred people or so who had; and she possessed no doubts at all about the creature's reality.

Back at the loch, I spent the afternoon watching from the northern shore, returning to Foyers for supper—to find that two of the guests had seen a curious V wake, earlier in the day, moving down the middle of the loch in a westerly direction. Questioning them closely, I found that neither witness had thought too seriously about it at the time, but the wash they described seemed to have been of considerable dimensions— without anything visible causing it.

I knew that in the spring there were large salmon in the loch, weighing 20–30 lb, but as a fisherman too, I also knew it would be virtually impossible for fish of this size to leave a wake visible at a range of nearly a thousand yards!

Much encouraged by this first dramatic indication I decided to redouble my efforts and remain completely alert, but in spite of the urgent need to maintain a watch on the water I still had a number of important visits to make.

I wanted to meet the Benedictine monks, who lived at Fort Augustus. At 8.30 p.m. that evening I knocked on the door at the entrance hall at St Benedict's Abbey, there to meet one of the residents, Father J. A. Carruth, a tall man of engaging personality.

I explained the purpose of my visit, and before many minutes had passed we were engaged in conversation, and I was soon to find the subject I had come to discuss was one of particular interest to Father Carruth, who had published a booklet* about it (a copy of which he kindly gave to me). Although he had never seen the Monster himself he was firmly convinced of its existence. We discussed the subject intently and came to agree that if the matter was approached with an open mind and the evidence studied carefully—particularly evidence at first hand—there

---

* *Loch Ness and its Monster.*

could be no reasonable doubt as to the existence of a very large and extraordinary creature, living in the loch.

I left the Abbey late that evening, gratified to have found that the conclusions I had drawn were shared by a man as sincere and intelligent as Father Carruth.

Fourth day

Daily log Thursday, April 21st.

5.10 a.m.	Got up.
5.40 a.m.– 9.10 a.m.	Watched Borlum Bay, and from Invermoriston.
9.30 a.m.–11.00 a.m.	Watched Foyers Bay.
11.00 a.m.–11.30 a.m.	Interview with Colonel Grant of Knockie.
11.45 a.m.–12.30 p.m.	Watched from southern shore—(area 4).
1.00 p.m.– 6.00 p.m.	Interview with Alex Campbell, Water Bailiff.
8.10 p.m.–	Filmed 'Monster' off Foyers river mouth.

RESULTS: Monster—approx. 20 ft of 16-mm film exposed at 840 yards: Survey—useful: Interviews—two eyewitnesses, excellent: Total viewing time: 11.45 hours.

In the past five days I have driven nearly 1,000 miles, and during the sorties round the loch had climbed most of the high places that looked down upon it—and I knew that fatigue was now my enemy. But, there was still much to be done and after the usual morning watch, as arranged, I met another witness: Colonel Grant of Knockie, who lived on his estate high up on the mountainside beyond the southern shore of the loch.

I was courteously received and we talked briefly. Colonel Grant told me that on one occasion in November of 1951 he had seen a great disturbance in the water about 150 yards off the shore at Inchnacardoch Bay, and then the back of some large animal appeared. It had dived, swimming just beneath the surface for a hundred yards or so, travelling at quite extraordinary speed, leaving a wash like that from a speed boat, breaking on the shore behind. As a result of this experience, he had no longer had any doubt about the presence of some very strange and powerful animal in the loch, but again, understandably, he preferred not to try to name it.

I thanked him for his assistance, and permission to watch the loch from the precipitous shore on his property. As I climbed away over the hilltops, carrying my equipment I thought about the interview. I had been much impressed by the Colonel's reserved account, which was so obviously factual.

Reaching the crest of a hill I set up the camera high above the water, the wind whipping and snatching at my clothing. Looking down on the great loch below I knew that unless it gave up its secret soon I must fail in my quest, because within 24 hours I would be making unwilling preparations for the long and tedious journey home.

That afternoon I continued to watch from Foyers Bay, and then travelled once more to Fort Augustus, to meet a man I felt sure would speak with authority on the subject—Alex Campbell, the water bailiff, whose story I had read so many months ago. I knew that he had worked as bailiff on the loch for many years.

Arriving at Fort Augustus I crossed the bridge over the river Oich, and turned down a side road towards the loch, and a few moments later knocked on the door of a cottage. The man who opened it spoke with the pleasantly distinct accent of the Highlander, and, inviting me inside, quickly put me at my ease.

Alex Campbell was quite unlike the bailiff I had imagined. He was a man in his fifties, of slight build and scholarly appearance, and as I had already explained the purpose of my visit the day before, on the telephone, he proceeded with his story without further delay or formality. Briefly he described again the occasion on which he had watched the animal floating on the surface, with its head and neck gracefully upraised above the water with a great length of body showing behind it—and how it had dived in a swirl when frightened by the noise of herring drifters. He spoke also of other occasions on which he had seen the creature. Once when he was out fishing from a boat, with a friend, the great humped back of the animal had risen slowly above the surface, only a few yards distant, and had then sunk again—much to their disquiet and astonishment. On another occasion, at a greater distance, he had seen two separate Monsters, rolling and splashing about on the surface, one of which clearly exhibited a pair of forward flippers.

He talked with reserve, and absolute sincerity, making no attempt to impress me or dramatize his account, and in so doing he was doubly impressive. Thus it was that in the quiet of this cottage by the loch, I knew I had met a man who spoke the truth. As he was the first person to whom I had talked who had *actually seen* the Monster's sinuous head and neck protruding above the water, I knew without any last tremor of doubt that the huge back could not be that of a whale, or a porpoise, or seal, or any other type of ordinary creature, that had somehow contrived to find a way into the loch.

I said goodbye to Alex Campbell, assured of the fact that I had found a friend on whom I could count for support in the future. I left the cottage at 7.30 p.m., and on the picturesque journey back to Foyers had time to re-assess the situation. In the light of what I had just been told, I decided to extend the hunt by a further day. I knew the Monster was a creature of flesh and blood, but more important, I believed it to be still alive. The quite unexplainable wake in the loch the previous day suggested this most strongly.

Exhilarated by the thought of this last minute reprieve from failure, I set up the camera on the hill behind the bay at Foyers and began to watch again, and for the thousandth time scanned from left to right with every conscious effort. The light began to fail, and then, quite suddenly, looking down towards the mouth of the river Foyers, I thought I could see a violent disturbance— a churning ring of rough water, centring about what appeared to be two long black shadows, or shapes, rising and falling in the water!

Without hesitation I focused the camera and methodically exposed twenty feet or so of film; and then, as the disturbance did not subside I decided to try and get a great deal closer. I drove quickly down the zigzag road to Foyers; past the aluminium works and across the grass of a football field. Jumping out I hurriedly stalked through the trees and bushes dotting the small peninsular of land leading out to the river mouth. Scarcely daring to breathe, with camera at the ready, I approached the very spot, expecting to meet the Monster face to face—but all I found was the smooth-flowing river and the windswept loch beyond it; the disturbance seemed to have completely disappeared.

I was not unduly surprised, though very much disappointed. It was clear that the Monster, in the time it had taken me to get to the peninsular had swum away: so after half an hour of hopeful waiting, in the rapidly fading light I returned to the hotel—and had a glass of beer to celebrate. I went to bed quite sure that the Monster, or part of it at least, was nicely in the bag!

Fifth day

Daily log April 22nd

6.00 a.m.	Got up.
6.30 a.m.– 9.20 a.m.	Watched from area 3.
9.30 a.m.– 2.30 p.m.	Watched from Foyers Bay. Set up and filmed scale posts at River mouth.
2.30 p.m.– 4.30 p.m.	Watched from boat, with salmon fisherman.
5.00 p.m.– 9.00 p.m.	Watched from Foyers Bay.

RESULTS: Monster—nil: Survey—shoreline study: Total watching time, 13 hours.

Relieved of the burden of anticipation, and the intolerable thought of defeat, I enjoyed a refreshing night's sleep; awoke without the aid of the alarm at 6 o'clock and travelling out along the road in an easterly direction, I climbed high up on the precipitous southern shore opposite Urquhart Castle and watched the loch until breakfast-time. It was a beautiful tranquil morning; the huge expanse of water lay spread out below like a giant's tablecloth, sparkling in the early sunlight, and as I sat gazing down upon it I was startled by the noise of stones tumbling down the mountainside. I looked up to see a roe deer bounding across the face of it—a lovely graceful creature, poised and alert, sure-footed on the almost precipitous slope; a very part of the natural scene surrounding it. I watched it disappear into a distant stand of fir trees and then looked back to the loch, conscious of the perfection about me.

Later in the day at Foyers I mapped the mouth of the river, and with the help of a boat charted its depths, using a weighted line and an adjustable fishing float; setting up some posts of measured length in the mud, I climbed to the point from which I had first seen the disturbance and took a number of covering pictures. I knew that the film would be of little scientific value unless some finite reference to scale could be included in it to provide a means of comparison.

While these operations were in progress I was helped by two local fishermen, who also lent me their boat and muscular assistance with every sign of goodwill. During my days at the loch I had found that the people who lived around its shores, the proud Highlanders, accepted my strange activities with no more than mild curiosity and on every occasion had offered me their friendship and advice. I like them, and envied their unhurried lives, and the magnificent countryside in which they lived.

In the afternoon, at the kind invitation of an ardent salmon fisherman, a retired sea captain, I went out trolling in a boat, and although we caught no fish it gave me an ideal opportunity to study a part of the shores of the loch and to watch from water level. From this excursion I learned two further lessons. A boat provided a means of studying parts of the shore of the loch which were otherwise invisible, but at actual water level the view over the surface, the detailed view, was very much restricted; and furthermore the movement of the boat itself prevented the use of a telephoto lens. All things considered, therefore, it was a very poor platform.

Sixth and last day of hunt

Daily log April 23rd, 1920

5.00 a.m.	Got up.
5.20 a.m.– 8.40 a.m.	Borlum Bay, and patrolled area 2.
9.00 a.m.– 9.04 a.m.	Filmed Monster for approx. 4 minutes at 1,300 yards increasing to 1,800 yards.
9.07 a.m.–10.00 a.m.	Watched from shore west of Foyers.
10.00 a.m.–12.00 a.m.	Filmed supporting sequences of boat.
12.30 p.m.	Lunch.
1.00 p.m.	Depart southwards. END OF HUNT.

FINAL RESULTS:
(1) Loch survey: 482 miles covered: loch perimeter studied.
(2) Total watching time: 73.00 hours.
(3) Interviews with eyewitnesses: 5.
Interviews with informed persons: 2.
(4) Monster: Approx. 20 ft 16-mm film exposed on disturbance at Foyers river mouth. 21.4.60.
Approx. 50 ft 16-mm film exposed on back of large animal opposite Foyers Bay. 23.4.60.

At dawn on this last day of the hunt, I got up and repeated the usual pre-breakfast activities; watching first Borlum Bay from the heights above, and then from the northern shore opposite the horse-shoe mark—waiting in hope to see the Monster climb out of the loch in the manner the rumour had suggested—but without avail. As the hours passed, I began to think of breakfast—

the delicious sound and smell of frying eggs and bacon plagued my imagination, and my very empty stomach. At last I could stand it no longer and a few minutes before the accustomed hour set off back to Foyers, driving through the mountains along the single track I had come to know so well; past the little Loch Tarff, and the turning to Knockie lodge, then up and down and around about in a switchback of turns and gradients; finally climbing the hill behind the bay at Foyers, at the top of which the loch is seen once more.

A little before I approached this point I thought about the camera lying cushioned on the back seat. I knew that on the way down to the hotel I must pass within sight of the loch for a period of twenty or thirty seconds but although I knew the rules about maintaining a state of instant readiness when any-where near the water, for a moment I was undecided. It seemed a lot of bother to mount the camera and tripod inside the car again for just these fleeting seconds, and I wanted breakfast badly. After a pause, when everything hung in balance, I decided to stick to the rigid drill which had become so much a matter of habit.

I stopped the car, and set up the tripod, next to the driver's seat, and putting up the camera adjusted the friction clamps for movement in pitch and traverse. I took a light reading, and adjusted the lens aperture, checking also the focus, the turret setting, the viewfinder parallax and frame, the ciné camera speed and motor. When all was in order I trained the camera out of the window in a slightly downwards direction, repeating the actions I had come to know as if by instinct.

I rolled the car slowly down the hill, with one hand on the tripod, glancing down towards the loch, stretched out in panoramic view two or three hundred feet below. The far shore, though just over a mile away, looked near enough to touch, and the black water between lay without a ripple. The sun shone brightly, its rays unimpeded by the clear mountain air. At a point approxi-mately halfway down the road to the hotel, looking out at the water, I saw an object on the surface about two-thirds of the way across the loch. By now, after so many hours of intensive watching, I was completely familiar with the effect that distance had on the scale of the local fishing-boats, nearly all of which were built on common lines, 15 ft or so in length. The first thing that struck me immediately about the object was that although it appeared to be slightly shorter than a fishing-boat, at the same distance, it stood *too high* out of the water; and furthermore, with the sun shining on it brightly it had a curious *reddish brown* hue about it which could be distinctly seen with the naked eye.

Unhurried, I stopped the car and raising my binoculars, focused their carefully.

The object was perfectly clear and now quite large. Although when first I had seen it, it lay sideways on, during the few seconds I had taken with the binoculars it seemed to have turned away from me. It lay motionless on the water, a long oval shape, a distinct mahogany colour. On the left flank a huge dark blotch could be seen, like the dapple on a cow. For some reason it reminded me of the back of an African buffalo—it had fullness and girth and stood well above the water, and although I could see it from end to

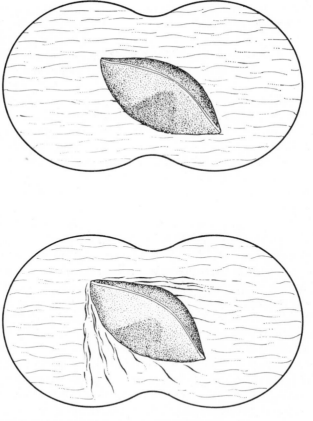

Figure 9   My sighting of the Monster, 23 April 1960.

end there was no visible sign of a dorsal fin. And then. Abruptly. It began to move. I saw ripples break away from the further end, and I knew at once I was looking at the extraordinary humped back of some huge living creature!

I dropped my binoculars, and turned to the camera, and with deliberate and icy control, started to film; pressing the button, firing long steady bursts of film like a machine gunner, stopping between to wind the clockwork motor. I could see the Monster through the optical camera sight (which enlarged slightly) making it appear very clear indeed; and as it swam away across the loch it changed course, leaving a glassy zigzag wake. And then it slowly began to submerge. At a point two or three hundred yards from the opposite shore, fully sub-merged, it turned abruptly left and proceeded parallel to it, throwing up a long V wash. It looked exactly like the tip of a submarine conning tower, just parting the surface, and as it proceeded westwards, I watched successive rhythmic bursts of foam break the surface—*paddle strokes:* with such a regular beat I instinctively began to count—one, two, three, four—pure white blobs of froth contrasting starkly against the black water surrounding, visible at 1,800 yards or so with the naked eye.

Awestruck, I filmed the beast as it proceeded westwards in a line as straight as an arrow, panning the camera to keep pace with it. I knew that as I had already exposed a length of film the day before there would not be much in reserve, and a quick look at the footage indicator proved this to be the case— I had only 15 ft remaining. Faced with an appalling decision, and only seconds in which to make it, I stopped filming. The Monster was now a long way off, and going at considerable speed in a westerly direction. I glanced at the second hand of my watch again—in 4 minutes the animal had swum nearly three-quarters of a mile, and was almost out of range; a mile and a half away at least. I dare not risk these last few precious feet of film, because at any moment I knew it might come to the surface again, or change direction, and come dashing back across the loch with head and neck upraised. It was the head and neck I wanted. I had now recorded the wake on 20–30 ft of film and could add nothing useful to it, so I decided on a sudden gamble— I knew it would be possible to drive the car across a field, right to the water's edge at a point to the west of lower Foyers and that in so doing in just a very few minutes, two or three at most, I could get nearly a thousand yards closer.

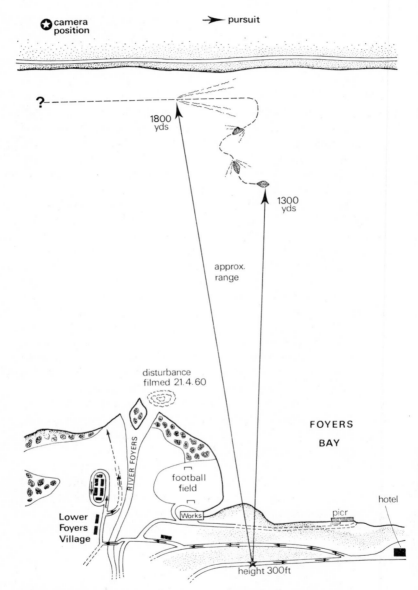

Figure 10 Sketch showing location of my sighting, 23 April 1960.

It was certainly worth the risk, and in seconds I folded up the tripod, and shot off down the steep zigzag road, going like a rocket, sounding the horn as I went, leaving a trail of dust. Over the bridge at the bottom, wheeling right I missed the entrance to the field, and cursing wildly carried on into a loop road round a group of houses, knowing it would prove the quickest way in which to double back.

I went round the tarmac circuit with tyres squealing, almost on two wheels, driving as I had never driven before in my life—and at the side of the road in front I saw a man look up, his face a mask of astonishment. Rounding the last bend and then down the track, I changed into lower gear and tore off across the grass, arriving at the shore in a matter of seconds later.

I jumped out eager to learn my fate; but one brief glance was enough to tell me I had lost both the race, and my exhilarating gamble—the loch was once again as tranquil as a pond. Climbing 30 ft or so up a bank I looked to left and right, searching the surface with binoculars for miles in each direction but there was nothing to be seen upon it; no sight or even sound of a fishing-boat, or other surface craft.

In the few minutes it had taken to race to the water's edge, the Monster had dived once more back into the depths, but before the dark waters closed over it, it had given up to me a part—a little part—of its quite uncanny secret; and although I now knew the hunt was really over, I also knew without any lingering shadow of doubt I had at last succeeded.

Through the magic lens of my camera I had reached out, across a thousand yards and more, *to grasp the Monster by the tail.*

7 Battle commences

Back at the hotel my news was well received by the other guests, most of whom, by now, had become infected with the virus of 'Monster fever', which is very catching. At first I had been received with polite indifference: tolerance, in some cases, but there were certainly one or two who thought I was a little mad. But as the hunt progressed and people saw I was not, they began to ask questions when I returned for meals, at the end of each successive sortie, and it was because of these questions and genuine signs of interest that I was able to resolve a personal problem in connection with the Monster, and decide on a course of action—to which I have since adhered.

When arriving first at the loch, surrounded by cameras and equipment, I had been conscious of a feeling almost of guilt, and a strong desire to tell everyone I was only an ornithologist, on the look out for rare species of birds—because I knew this to be a very usual excuse. It is quite extraordinary how many reports about the Monster have come from ardent 'ornithologists' in the past, and it demonstrates a very natural human reaction; but I decided to tell people what I knew about the subject, everything about it, at every opportunity, and try to persuade them to study it themselves. In short, I started a sort of private crusade. In the past there had been so much running and hiding, and dishonesty around the loch, I knew it was time to start facing up to the facts, and the best way to do this was to start myself from the very beginning.

I did: and from that moment on, if people asked me what on earth I was doing, I told them outright I was 'looking for the Loch Ness Monster'—and I tried to tell them why, as well, if I had the time. It proved to be the right policy.

After breakfast I spoke to the proprietor about getting a boat to go out on the loch, so that I could film it as it steered the same course the Monster had taken. I knew that without a comparison of this kind the film would be of little scientific value, and yet with it the opposite would be true. The boat would provide a datum from which the Monster could be measured in terms of size, speed, and the sort of wake it made. I knew that this was absolutely necessary.

Hugh Rowand appreciated the need for this comparison at once, and without hesitation offered to do the job himself. This was generous, because I needed someone to steer and interpret the signals I intended to make with a flag, from the point where the film had been taken.

While Hugh prepared to launch the boat and installed the 5-horse power motor, I scribbled out a briefing with a copy for myself, defining the course to take and the sequence of turns and actions. On it I made out the necessary list of visual signals, so that when we were separated by a mile or so of water we might still understand each other clearly. When everything was ready and we both understood the signal code, Hugh climbed into the boat and sat in the stern, canting the motor clear of the rocky bottom. I gave a shove, and it floated out stern first, and as I climbed back up the mountainside to the hotel I heard the motor splutter into life, and looking round, watched the boat slowly gathering way.

Back at the filming point I tied a white shirt to the end of a branch, in preparation, and watched fascinated as the 14-ft craft, now no bigger than a water beetle, made its way slowly across the loch leaving an elegant trail of ripples, fanning out on either side. The motor buzzed like a bumble-bee and drowned any possible chance of shouted words between us; and I was glad of the flag which retained our vital intelligence link. Hugh sat facing me and I could see the sunlight shining off his face, and the shiny aluminium motor casing.

It was a curious sensation, watching the boat crawl across the loch getting even smaller, and I began to realize the size and power of the animal I had seen. A couple of wags with the flag, to the left, put the boat back on course, and when it reached the approximate position where I had first seen the Monster I exposed a few feet of film. Then, as arranged, two or three hundred yards distant from the far shore the boat turned abruptly left and proceeded up the loch, following the course the animal had taken when just beneath the surface. I shot more film, and then waved another signal. The plan was working well. While the boat came back across the loch I opened the door of the car and took a flashlight picture, showing how the camera had been mounted inside, and then quickly filmed the boat again, stationary in the place where I had first seen the disturbance off the mouth of the

Foyers river. Waving a last 'come home' signal, I jumped into the car and made my way down the hill, turning right past an aluminium works at the bottom. As the boat coursed along at full throttle, sailing parallel to the shore, I paced it with the car, glancing at the speedometer. It was doing exactly seven miles an hour.

A few minutes later I was helping to heave the boat back out of the loch. Back at the hotel I sealed the camera with sticky paper, across which the Rowands signed, as witnesses. Half an hour later I said goodbye, and set off for Fort Augustus where I had one more call to make—the Post Office. There I concocted a lengthy cable which I sent to the directors of the British Museum, recording the fact that on 21 and 23 April 1960 I had exposed so many feet of film, through such and such a lens, with such and such a camera, on the 'phenomenon' known as the Loch Ness Monster, promising that in due course I would report on the result. I did this because the Museum represented the highest zoological authority in the country and I felt they ought to be the first people to know about it. This last duty fulfilled, I set off on the long journey southward, realizing I would not arrive at my brother's farm in Northumberland until two or three in the morning. I drove tensely without a glance at the mountain scenery sweeping by, conscious still of the same driving force, the compelling energy that had kept me on my feet through the days of the hunt. If the film was any good at all it would have to be shown to scientists in a manner that did not excite publicity, because I knew that the two did not mix well together. With the confusion of doubt and prejudice that swirled around the Monster, I realized that even a convincing strip of film would probably be received with chilling reserve by professional men, whose very reputations would depend on not being easily fooled. There was also the problem of my own status as an engineer, which did not qualify me to speak with authority on matters of zoology—and why should anyone take me, or my word for granted? For all they knew I might be a fraud, or practical joker.

The more I thought about the problem, the more certain I became it was going to be a battle without any easy hopes of victory; and there was yet another problem which had to be anticipated. People had already said the film would be worth a fortune, and although I was disinclined to believe them too readily there was always the possibility they might be right, and it would thus be well to try and decide exactly what to do about it in advance.

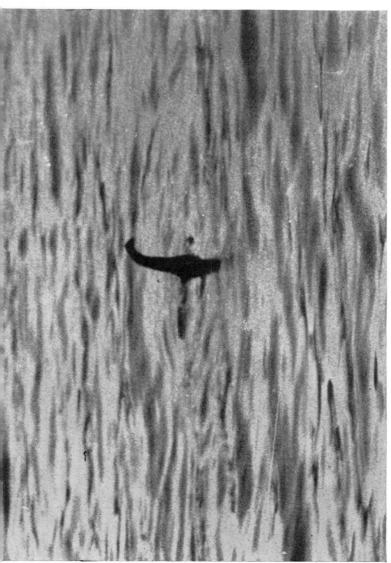

1 The surgeon's photograph. This picture was taken in 1934 at a range of 200-300 yards with a quarter-plate camera and a telephoto lens. It is still a source of much argument.

2 The picture obtained by Mr H. L. Cockrell from a canoe, early one morning in autumn 1958. The hump appeared to be about 4 ft in length.

3 This photo, taken in late summer 1955 by Mr P. A. Macnab, provides a precise scale: Castle Urquhart's tower stands exactly 64 ft above the ground. Note the wake. The account reads 'seeing a disturbance in the water . . . I took a chance and changed lenses, conscious of "something" big, undulating and moving at 8-12 knots; I snapped . . . just as the creature was sounding.' Exakta 127 camera, 6-inch lens, hand held at f8, 1/100th sec.

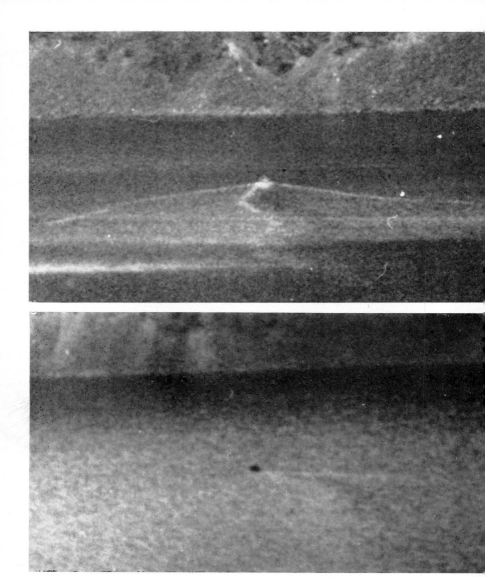

Enlarged stills from the author's film, taken 23 April 1960.

4a A 14ft boat with a 5-horsepower outboard travelling at 7 m.p.h. Note distinct bow wave and propeller wake.
4b The monster's hump shortly after starting to move. It is already beginning to submerge. Note different wake pattern. Range approximately 1,600 yards.

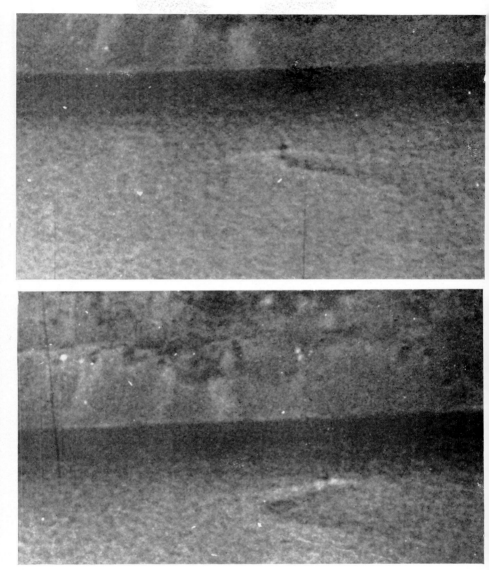

The value of the film lies chiefly in its portrayal of movement, but there is much to be learned from a careful examination of these stills.

5a Monster swings to right, still travelling slowly.
5b Zig-zag wake develops; the animal is now almost submerged.

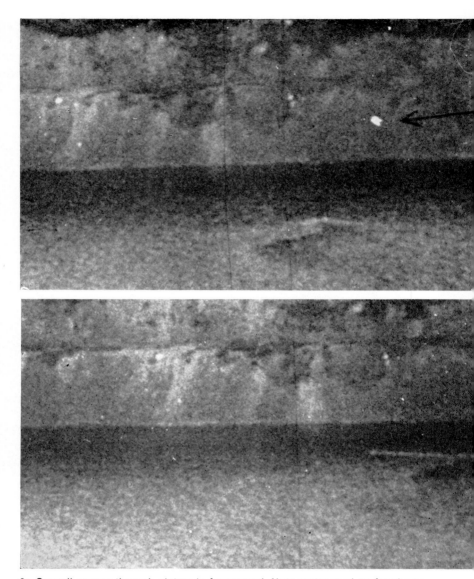

6a Seagull passes through picture in foreground. Note motor road on far shore: it really is Loch Ness.
6b Monster, now fully submerged, makes an abrupt turn to the left. Range about 1,800 yards.

7a Travelling at greater speed, at least 10 m.p.h., the Monster leaves a very considerable wash. Vehicle in background could be 15-20 ft long.
7b Same boat, same speed and wash; compare the difference.

8 In 1970 teamwork produced results with a side-scan sonar made by Klein Associates. Left to right: Robert Rines, president of the Academy of Applied Science, Martin Klein, designer of the equipment (both from U.S.A.), and the Author.

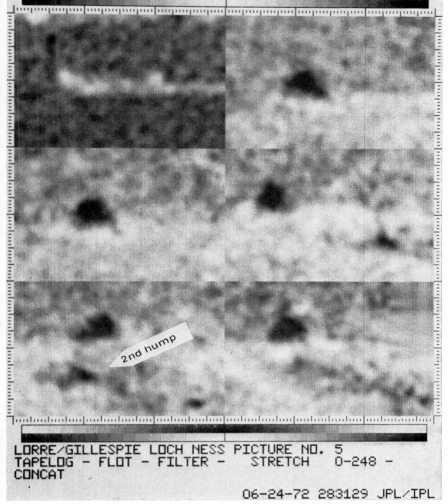

2nd hump

LORRE/GILLESPIE LOCH NESS PICTURE NO. 5
TAPELOG - PLOT - FILTER -   STRETCH   0-248 -
CONCAT

06-24-72 283129 JPL/IPL

9 Final proof of reality of my 1960 film came from the computer study made of it by NASA's Jet Propulsion Laboratories in Pasadena, California, in 1972—when a second hump is shown to break surface momentarily. Read frames top left to right. First is of boat.

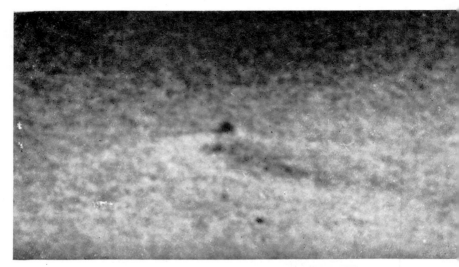

10 *Above* A much enlarged still from my 1960 film; hold the picture at arm's length and compare it with Hugh Rowand's sketch (Fig. 15).

11 *Below* 'The Monster's claw'—or a crocodile's foot?

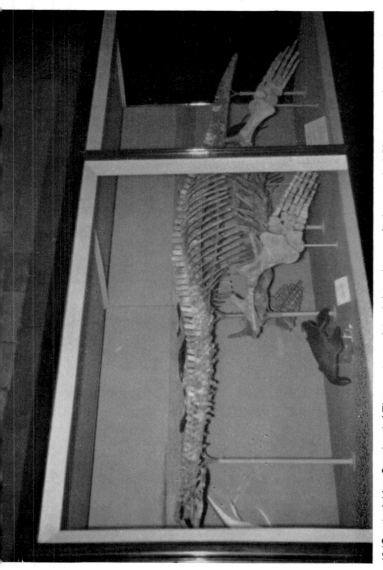

12 'Cryptocleidus Oxoniensis.' The most complete skeleton known of a long necked Plesiosaur—found in a clay pit near Peterborough. Compare the shape with that seen in Mr Cockrell's photograph.

13 This is the photograph taken from the deck of the yacht *Finola*, by Mr Lowrie when passing through Loch Ness, summer 1960.

If money had been the purpose of my visit to the loch, no doubt I would have been overjoyed at the thought of selling the film to the highest bidder; but as it was not, the prospect of a sudden flood of wealth proved almost an embarrassment—though a not unpleasant thought. Finally, however, I hit upon a compromise. I would not seek wealth for its own sake, and if I made anything out of the film, or from articles about it, the proceeds would go first of all towards proper equipment, and the cost of future expeditions. The cameras I possessed were inadequate, with the exception of the Bolex and 5 in. lens, which had been lent to me for the occasion. If I was to try my luck again at a future date I would need the very best equipment.

Thinking back to the episode of filming I realized the Monster had behaved itself extremely well, meeting the theoretical speci-fication on almost every count. It had appeared in the early morning at a place where it was commonly seen—Foyers Bay, where, in point of fact, a Gaelic legend states explicitly that 'water bulls are always to be found'. It was the right shape and colour, a huge reddish brown triangular hump. At first when swimming slowly, it had zigzagged about as if undecided where to go; then, when just below the surface, it travelled as straight as an arrow at greater speed, disregarding the passage of traffic along the nearby motor road. Both these characteristics had been reported in the past.

Altogether it had performed in a most obliging manner, and although the film had been shot at extreme range, and the Monster had swum in the wrong direction and failed to expose its neck, I had no complaints against it. I had caught it by its tail, and no power on earth would make me let go of it.

By now I had reached the Ballachulish ferry, the quaint little boats splashing their way across the entrance to Loch Leven, and later drove through the towering haunted cleft of Glencoe; its chill winds whispering of black and evil deeds in centuries gone by—and then, by slow degree, out into the flat lands once more, into the pall of soot and smoke, amongst rows and rows of houses—the home and working place of very many people.

On Sunday evening, 24 April, I arrived home to enjoy a family welcome. I had already spoken to my wife about the film, and she was, of course, delighted. In her own way, she had contributed much to the success of the venture and understood its meaning and significance.

At the first opportunity I made contact with Kodak Limited,

and arranged for the film to be processed and copied with every care and attention, and in this the works manager, Mr Coppin, offered invaluable assistance. He witnessed the breaking of the seals and recorded the film identification numbers, both on the original and copy films and, fittingly enough, shared with me the first projected viewing.

It proved to be a very tense business and as the film flickered on to the screen I watched it in dismay. The first few momentary sequences were badly under-exposed, showing boats and steamers moving through the water in different parts of the loch, which I had filmed deliberately, exposing a few frames on each to act as scaling markers. Then, running on for several minutes, the film portrayed the disturbance I had seen at the mouth of the Foyers river. At first sight it *did* look quite convincing, as though it might be caused by some powerful creature thrashing about underwater, but as the film ran on it became apparent it was no more than the wash and swirl of waves around a hidden shoal, caused by a sudden squall of wind. A second sequence taken the following day, with the loch in calmer mood, proved this to be the case without a doubt. Under the conditions of fading light and fatigue, I had in fact been fooled completely.

By now the film had run for more than half its length—but then the picture changed, with dramatic suddenness. It threw into focus the strange humped back of the Monster, moving through the water exactly as I had watched it: slowly submerging, leaving a zigzag wake before turning abruptly left to proceed down the loch like a miniature submarine.

The film ran out, but we wound it back and ran it through again, watching carefully. It was on this second viewing I realized that although it recorded the Monster I had seen in essential detail it sadly lacked the colour, the contrast and perspective which had been so apparent at the loch. The shabby little black and white image that traced its way across the screen, though correct in shape and movement was indeed a poor imitation of what I had witnessed. In spite of that, it did provide the evidence needed, the proof of what I had seen myself in real life. More important still the two short filmed sequences of the boat steering a similar course provided the comparison of wash, of scale and speed, so absolutely vital.

I left Kodak feeling cheerful enough, and in the weeks that followed showed the film to a number of scientific people, specialists of different kinds of senior standing, and also to a naturalist with whom I had corresponded. He was in fact one of the first people to see the film and, I think, appreciate its true significance and he did what he could to arouse official interest. It was not an easy task, and as time went by I realized the best I could hope to do at this early stage was to kindle people's interest sufficiently to start them on their own enquiring trail—nosing out the facts and stories and thus finding their own way to conviction. But, inevitably, it was a process that took time, and I had to admit my private disappointment. The one reaction I had not expected to meet was that of *apathy*, because the film demonstrated something of quite extraordinary interest—a huge animate object moving about in a freshwater lake cut off from the sea, in which there could, in theory, be nothing larger than salmon: a creature with a strange hump on its back, without a fin, capable of producing a wash greater than that from a Greenland whale!

This, I felt should be more than sufficient to prompt an immediate on-the-spot enquiry, with adequate equipment—but there were no signs of any such investigation or the funds to make one possible. For a time it baffled me completely, and I began to suspect that short of serving the Monster up on a dinner plate with a sprig of parsley on it, there was little one could do to get officialdom to act; but on further consideration, I decided not to be impatient. The majority of people with whom I was dealing were concerned, in one way or another, with a long established science—that of zoology—in which for very many years past the natural order of things and the animal life of this planet had been both well studied and understood, and in which discoveries were today measured in terms of minor variations of species which were already known. As long ago as 1812, Baron Georges Cuvier had stated with authority, 'there is little hope of discovering new species of large quadrupeds!'

The fact that from then on a long succession of major discoveries proved the existence of some of the largest quadrupeds ever found on earth, did not mean that people anticipated any such discoveries today. Over the last fifty years only three or at most four large four-legged animals had been discovered, and to expect any sudden departure from this established line of thinking would be entirely mistaken.

But people seemed to be very complacent about the Monster. If it was exciting to me, an engineer, surely it ought to be ten times as exciting to zoologists—but the reactions I had so far encountered were so very staid that I began to wonder whether I might not profitably introduce the film in future with a stick of dynamite—like the one I had heard go off on the shores of the loch with such a delightful ear-splitting bang!

By now it was early June, and the film had remained a secret for nearly seven weeks. The dynamic reaction I had expected did not seem to be forthcoming, and in contrast to my effort at the loch, with such a specific object in view, I now seemed doomed to wait about hoping for something to happen; and worse, as I had now been asked to keep the film a secret indefinitely until a closer sequence was obtained, the opportunity of raising funds to cover expenses and the cost of new equipment had disappeared.

The expenses of the trip had turned out to be heavy, and I could ill afford them; I had underestimated the travelling costs, and by the time I had paid all the bills I was somewhat out of pocket. All things considered, the programme was not going well, and although I agreed to keep the film a secret indefinitely, it was a miserable decision to have to make. I was really rather proud of it.

Then, a newspaper reporter came to the door claiming he knew all about the film and the names of those connected with it. He made it abundantly clear that unless I told him the story he would very soon find someone who would! The situation was now entirely different and I wondered how to face it. If I continued to keep silent the story would come out anyway, no doubt distorted. The Monster would probably become a laughing stock again, but after so much effort this could not be allowed to happen. There was only one thing to do. If it was no longer possible to keep the film a secret I had to do the opposite—to show it to everyone at the first opportunity, and tell the truth about it; and this I resolved to do. After weeks of indecisive action it was nice to grasp the reins in my own hands once more, certain of direction; and besides, I was sick of all the secrecy, and the more I thought about it, the more certain I became it was the root of the trouble at Loch Ness. Over the past twenty-eight years there had been so much secrecy, and sitting on the fence and dodging the issues that for all its sophistication and twentieth-century knowledge, science had in fact behaved towards the Monster, the 'impossible', exactly as in Galileo's day—it had turned its back upon it. Such being the case the sooner people began to stick up for the truth about it, the better it would be.

As soon as it was possible I got on to an established firm of film distributors in London, and within hours a programme had been planned.

Arrangements were put in hand for an interview, and commentary on the film for release on television news around the world—an appointment was fixed with the director of a national daily paper; contact was established with the 'Panorama' people on B.B.C. television, and a written account and stills from the film were prepared for release to newspapers in other countries.

I had asked for action, and had got it, in no small measure. For this I had to thank two dynamic and honest individuals at the offices of United Press International, two Americans, full of fun and ideas; an absolute tonic to morale!

I had guessed that the greatest potential threat lay in mistaken or exaggerated newspaper stories. There was only one way to meet it, and that was to go right to the top, explain the situation and ask for co-operation. Several national newspapers had in the past treated the subject with consideration, and as the *Daily Mail* was no exception I had no doubts about offering them the story. As a result of the interview I was duly reported with good sense and impartiality on the morning of 13 June 1960. Reference was made to the 'Panorama' show the same evening, so that readers had the opportunity to tune in and judge the film for themselves.

It was a relief to have taken the newspaper hurdle with such an easy stride, and once the story appeared in print it lost its exclusive value. This meant I could go forward to the next jump, the unnerving TV programme, knowing that the Monster's reputation was still undamaged.

The first interview with the 'Panorama' team proved a success. They treated the matter with intelligence and understanding and although I could be sure the film and my own evidence would be treated with critical detachment, they would also give me every opportunity to prepare a case—and what was more important, they offered to *enlarge* the film as much as possible, and transpose it from the original 16-mm. strip to 35-mm—a tricky laboratory process.

I was impressed with their efficiency and determination to adjudicate fairly, even to the extent of flying their questioner, Jim Mossman, up to the loch to make his own enquiries and satisfy himself I had taken the film from the place described— but however well the preparations were laid I could not hope to judge the outcome. This was to be the crucial test. The film would be judged by millions of people, and upon their reaction hung in balance the Monster's reputation; that delicate thing which had to be guarded so jealously! I knew very well that if the film was not convincing, or if I failed to present my arguments properly, the result could be disastrous—but on the evening of 13 June I saw the enlarged version run through on the television screen for the first time, and was very much encouraged. Enlarged first two, and then four times, the humped back of the Monster could be clearly seen before it began to submerge. As it swam just underwater, close to the further shore, it was possible to make out a definite paddling action, swirling the water back in the manner of a breast stroke swimmer. But perhaps the most striking improvement on the original film (which was by no means spectacular) was the increase in definition and contrast resulting from a characteristic inherent in TV cameras, which produce a contrasted image on the screen from a low-contrast original. As the film was somewhat under-exposed, and therefore short of contrast, it suited television well.

I was delighted to see that Alex Campbell had been invited down, and had no doubt he would speak with the same imperturbable manner I had found so convincing when I met him at the loch.

The programme was, as usual, in three parts with the 'Monster' interview last of all, which meant we had to sit and wait in anxious anticipation. I did not enjoy this at all, and the confusion of lights and weird TV cameras, creeping about on rubber wheels, reaching out and up and down, goggling at us with a multitude of eyes, did nothing to ease the tension, and I was glad when the waiting time was over. The twelve minutes of question and answer; the film, and discussion of what the object could be, passed quickly and smoothly without embarrassment. Campbell spoke of his own experiences, of his view of the head and neck and the astounding speed of which the Monster was capable. I did my best to analyse the film step by step, pointing out the obvious difference between the wake of the boat, with its pronounced bow wave and line of propeller wash, and that of the Monster with its glassy V wash—but it was really unnecessary to talk, because the film spoke for itself, and I concentrated instead on a number of other points.

The film, I argued, clearly demonstrated the presence of some large animate object in Loch Ness, which in view of all the other evidence should now be properly investigated. I made no attempt to try to name the object because I knew that as I did not speak with authority on matters of zoology it would be a mistake to try. Instead I showed a model of a Monster, made out of clay and carrying the same peculiar mark on its flank which I had seen so distinctly. The model was no more than a prototype, based on average statistics, showing the animal with three humps instead of the two most commonly reported, or the single hump that appeared in the film. A few days previously when building it, I had thought carefully about these humps and decided to include them only as an indication of the fact that they were seen on occasion. As future events were to prove, I might equally well have left them out.

The programme ran to its conclusion, timed to the second. When it was over Richard Dimbleby spoke to me and said that the film had convinced him the object we had watched was not a boat, or anything else he could think of—in short that it was quite unexplainable. This was good news, because Dimbleby was a man of very wide experience, a professional adjudicator used to summing up the pros and cons of controversial subjects. I felt this definite assurance spoke well for the film and its chance of success, and in this I was not mistaken. Within a few days mail began to come in from all parts of the country, from people in every walk of life: lords and commoners, and from amongst all these letters there was but one dissenting voice—a man who rather gamely offered to explain the Monster by a meteorological theory.

There could be no doubt about it, the film had proved convincing and the Monster was firmly reinstated as an object of serious interest. I was happy about it; after so much disappointment we had gained ground, and having now done my best with the film, I could concentrate once more on my own particular studies. Having established the Monster was real and alive, I had got to stage three in the plan of investigation—the 'what the devil is it?' stage, which promised to be intriguing.

By now I had the name of the man who claimed to have seen the beast on the shore, earlier in the year, and those of other people who had seen it at a distance of only a few yards with its head and neck out of water. If I wanted to study the Monster in further detail the first thing would be to talk to these people. It would mean another expedition.

8 Review of interesting cases

1 Past evidence confirmed

Account no. 1a—from a letter to me dated 26 June 1960.
Witness: Mrs Marjory Moir, Inverness.
Date of occurrence: October 1936.

Your film of the research work on the Loch Ness Monster,
shown recently in 'Panorama', was so interesting that I must
write to convey my congratulations, and to tell you my own
story about the 'Monster'; I shall begin about sixty
years back.

My father, who was born and brought up on a farm high
up on the hills overlooking Loch Ness, used to tell me that
when he was a small boy and got into mischief on the farm,
the servants often frightened him by saying, 'The water
Kelpie will get you'. The memory of hearing this has
remained with me ever since.

When I was a small child my older sisters often took me
for walks in that delightful part of Inverness known as The
Islands. In one part of The Islands the river Ness divides,
and there is a narrow stream which has a waterfall. As I
passed this waterfall, I associated it with my father's
'Water Kelpie', and it was with fear and trembling that I ran
past it—the noise of the water rushing over the boulders
and the quick flashing lights on it were to me a 'Water
horse'. That memory has also remained.

The years passed. I married and went abroad. In 1932
returning from leave, I was reading the news bulletin one
day on the notice board of a Royal Mail steamer in the
South Atlantic; there was a brief paragraph about a strange
creature having been seen in Loch Ness. So here it was—
my father's Water Kelpie; my water-horse; The Loch Ness
Monster. Local newspapers, sent to us from time to time,
often had news of this strange creature and my interest
became more intense.

In 1936 I was again back in Inverness. One October

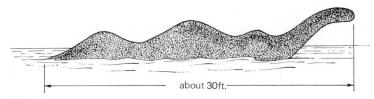

about 30ft.

Figure 11   Sketch drawn by Mrs M. Moir of her sighting, October 1936.

afternoon a friend took my sister, mother-in-law, my young daughter and myself for a little trip by car to Foyers. On the return journey, at a place where the road runs very close to the loch, about three miles from Foyers, my sister suddenly shouted, 'Look, there's the Monster'. We all got out of the car and ran to the water's edge. There, before us, at a distance of one third the width of the loch away from us, was this wonderful creature. It was a perfect view, if we had a camera the most convincing picture of the Monster ever taken could have been obtained, but alas! we had neither camera nor binoculars.

The sky was grey, the loch was grey and the silhouette of the creature was a very dark grey against the lighter background. A perfect setting. There were three distinct humps, a long slender neck ending in a small head, and the overall length appeared to me thirty feet approximately. I could see no details of eyes, mouth, etc. but the outline was all beautifully clear—the three humps, head and neck— (I shall enclose a sketch for you). The middle hump was the highest, the one behind the neck the smallest, and the in-between size was at the back, sloping in a graceful line down to, and under, the water. The creature was quite stationary, and often dipped its head into the water, either feeding or amusing itself.

We watched in awe and amazement, for about 5–8 minutes; then suddenly it swung round away from the shore, and shot across the loch at a terrific speed, putting up a wash exactly similar to that I saw in your film. All the time I could see a small dark spot, perhaps the highest hump, perhaps the head. When it eventually came to rest I noticed the *humps had disappeared*; the back was now more or less straightened out, but the neck and head were as before. The creature was in full view for 14 minutes. I have no idea how much of the body was underneath the water, but what we saw was a huge creature, evidently very powerful, graceful and quite at ease on and in the water. A thrilling experience—I actually saw the Loch Ness Monster, resting, and travelling at speed, I saw the humps, then the straightened out back, my 'Water Horse' in truth at last.

You can now—I hope—understand why your film was of such absorbing interest to me, so much in it was exactly what I saw and remember so vividly. One more thing—the composite picture* shown at the end of your film was the same in every detail as the Monster I saw in October, 1936, even to the approximate length.

Many people have seen this creature, it does exist. I watched it at quite a comfortable distance for nearly a quarter of an hour, I was fascinated, and now know that the 'Water Kelpie' which so frightened my father many years ago was not an imaginary bogey, but a real live creature . . .
P.S. When the B.B.C. did a T.V. programme on the Loch Ness Monster, over two years ago, I was invited to be interviewed. At the end of the programme I was standing near the edge of the loch, the diver in charge of the diving operations appeared out of the water just beside me. He removed his headgear and said, 'That was a nasty job, a most sinister place. I do not want to go diving in there again. I have been down in waters all around Britain, and always there was light to a considerable depth, and little things all around, full of life; but down there it was dark and lifeless.'

Comment This account from Mrs Moir (who is a sincere and educated person) is unusual in that it provides so much varied information of interest about the Monster. First there is the legendary 'water kelpie' and the fear it instilled in the mind of a child all those years ago. Then there is the Monster of reality, the long snake-like neck, the little head, its great size, and the extraordinary humps capable of actually changing shape; the sudden dash across the loch—and then in contrast, the strange words from the experienced diver; sentiments that have been expressed by others who have ventured into the black and eerie depths of the loch. All these details fit the general picture, but enthralling though her written account may be, it is still more impressive to hear it from Mrs Moir herself because, like others

* Actually the half-section model.

Figure 12   Sketch drawn by Mrs Greta Finlay of her sighting, 20 August 1952.

who have seen the Monster in real life, it is an experience which has affected her profoundly, and which she will not forget.

Account no. 1b—from a letter to me dated September 1960.
Witness: Mrs Greta Finlay, Inverness.
Date of occurrence: 20 August 1952.

It is necessary to introduce this account with an explanatory note. Mrs Greta Finlay, a housewife and resident of Inverness, happened to be near the north-east shore of the loch near to Aldourie pier off Tor Point, when the Monster appeared quite literally a few yards away in the water. She told me she 'could have hit it with a pebble.' Her small son was with her at the time, hoping to enjoy a little fishing!

> I was sitting outside the caravan when I heard a continual splashing in the water. After several moments passed and realizing this was not the usual wash from a boat I walked round. To my surprise I saw what I believe to be the Loch Ness Monster. My son and I stood looking at this creature in amazement. Although I was terrified, we stood and watched until it submerged, which it did very quickly causing waves to break on the shore. We had an excellent view as it was so close to the shore. Its skin was dark in colour and looked very tough. The neck was long and held erect. The head was about the same width as the neck. There were two projections from it, each with a blob on the end. This was not a pleasant experience. I certainly never want to see the Monster again. My son had drawn several sketches, one of which I enclose.

Comment When I talked to Mrs Finlay about her experience I noticed that she found the memory of it very disturbing, and she freely admitted that at the time she was paralysed with fear; and the experience so much affected her small son that he gave up fishing altogether. Apparently the animal they saw was small by 'Monster' standards, the visible parts being about 15 ft in length.

This reaction of fear is most interesting, and one I have come across in men as well as women, all of whom readily admit to it. There appears to be little doubt that at close quarters the Monster is a formidable creature, the head and neck of which has been described to me as like that of a 'giant anaconda', 10–12 ft in length, tapering from a very wide base, out towards the head. The man who described it in these words saw the head and neck alone, at a range of 20–30 yards and noticed the peardrop glistening eyes set near the top of the head. The effect this appalling 'apparition' had, as it gracefully approached the shore, was quite dynamic on both himself and two other men. Together they beat an undignified retreat—and these were strong men of mature years!

Altogether this is a very interesting report, though the printed word cannot adequately describe Mrs Finlay's personal reaction to the experience, or the memory of it, which is almost that of revulsion. This, it may be remembered, is the reaction noted by Commander Gould when talking to the Spicers who claimed to have seen the Monster crossing the road near Dores.

Account no. 1c—from a letter dated 16 October 1960.

Witness: Mr Alexander Campbell, water bailiff for over forty-five years at Loch Ness.
Date of occurrence: May 1934.

I enclose a sketch of what I saw away back in 1934 (my first view of the Monster), and the description of the incident is as follows: I was standing at the mouth of the river Oich (which flows past my door) one beautiful morning that summer—May, if I remember aright, and was gazing across the loch in the direction of Borlum Bay. Suddenly my attention was drawn to a strange object that seemed to shoot out of the calm waters almost opposite the Abbey boathouse. As you can see from the sketch, the swanlike neck reached six feet or so above the water at its highest point, and the body, a darkish grey glistening with moisture was *at least*

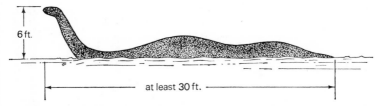

Figure 13   Sketch drawn by Alex Campbell of his sighting, May 1934.

30 ft. long. I gauged this carefully in my mind's eye by placing two ordinary rowing boats of 15 ft. overall length end to end, and I don't think I was far wrong, because I have had lots of experience of that sort of thing, because I have lived on the shores of the loch all my life—apart from the last war years. Still watching and wondering if I would have time to run for my camera, I heard the noise of the engines of two herring drifters (they call them trawlers in England) which were proceeding down the lower basin of the Caledonian Canal, which enters the loch almost alongside the Abbey boathouse. The animal certainly must have heard, or sensed, the approach of these vessels too, for I saw it turn its head in an apprehensive way, this way and that, and, apparently being timid, it then sank rapidly out of sight, lowering the neck in doing so, and leaving a considerable disturbance on the mirror-like surface of the loch. The animal would have been some 400 yards from where I stood, possibly less, and I had a very clear view of it which lasted several minutes.

Comment   There is little that need be said about this account which is clear enough in itself, although it would be a good thing, perhaps, to point out once more that with all his years of experience on Loch Ness, Alex Campbell is very well able to judge the scale of objects seen upon the water. Another point of interest is the Monster's apparent awareness of sound, or perhaps vibration, in the water, and the alert way in which it moved its head, because this is a characteristic reported by many.

Account no. 1d—from a letter dated 14 September 1960.
This account, which is very brief, does not involve a witness, nor does it concern any previous published report, but it is of interest from a purely historical point of view and was made available to me by a friend who saw the film. It reads:

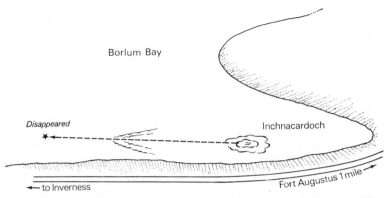

Figure 14   Sketch drawn by Colonel P. Grant of his sighting, October 1955.

This is the information I promised you. My friend's grandmother, Mrs Elspeth McKenzie of Brora used to tell the story of a strange beast in Loch Ness. She said it appeared in the loch at times and then it seemed to go away. At that time, they said there was an outlet to the sea from under the loch, by which the beast used to come and go.

My friend's mother would have been 89 if she was alive today and it was *her* mother who used to talk about it, though I do not know whether she actually saw the beast herself.

Comment   Although the legend of the 'beast in Loch Ness' goes back far into history, this is the earliest personal record I have been able to get hold of, suggesting the Monster was in evidence at least a hundred years ago.

Account no. 1e—from a letter dated 18 December 1960.

Witness: Colonel Patrick Grant, Knockie Estate, Loch Ness.
Date of occurrence: October 1955.

On a still frosty morning in October of 1955 I was driving a car from Fort Augustus to Invermoriston. Whilst close to the loch at Inchnacardoch Bay I saw a great commotion in the water about 100 to 200 yards from the road. There could be no possible doubt about this as the bay was a dead flat calm at this time. By the time I had pulled up the car the splashing had ceased but I could see the length of some black object above the surface like a floating log, ten or fifteen feet long. I was not high enough to get any idea of its breadth, but the topline was quite straight.

After a short time (under a minute), the object suddenly started swimming eastwards, parallel with the shore and very near the surface though submerged. It moved at a great pace and made a heavy wash like a fast motor boat. After going 200 or 300 yards, the wash stopped quite suddenly and the creature must have dived, as it disappeared completely and I never saw it again.

Note: The *Inverness Courier* published a few lines about my sighting, and this may be of some interest to you because it confirmed that the Monster was sighted from another point— but at the same time and place by a Mrs K—— wife of the doctor at Fort Augustus.

Comment   The part of this report which I find most interesting is the description of the animal swimming just beneath the surface leaving a great wash, which suddenly petered out when it dived. This wash is precisely what the film shows, and it is of interest to know the manner in which it probably ended, because that is something I missed when racing in pursuit.

2   More recent cases

With two exceptions, the occurrences referred to in this section have taken place since the film was obtained in April of 1960.

The first report is from Hugh Rowand, proprietor of Foyers Hotel, and concerns an appearance in the spring of 1958. I have included it because I am certain of its veracity, and the accuracy of the detail in the sketch.

My wife and I together with two friends were seated on our lawn overlooking the loch early in the spring, when my attention was drawn to a quite large 'fin' shaped object in the water a few yards off Sand Point. The object appeared triangular in shape and we thought it might possibly be a large piece of concrete 'shuttering' washed down possibly from the river Moriston—after operations by the Hydro Electric Board.

However, as the object was stationary, no further interest was taken in it, but a few moments later it suddenly came to life, literally rocketed across the loch towards Drumnadrochit, for a distance of possibly 400–500 yards and then submerged.

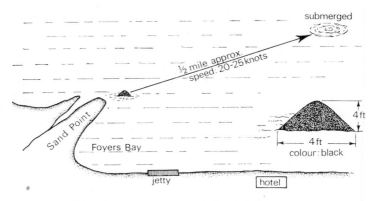

Figure 15   Sketch drawn by Hugh Rowand of his sighting, spring 1958.

The most astonishing part of this performance being the speed at which it moved, which at a very rough guess, I would estimate at something between 20–25 knots! Whilst of course it is difficult to assess speeds with any degree of accuracy from the position in which we were placed, the known speeds of various boats we see from time to time can be used comparatively. None of us would like to hazard a guess as to what it was!

Comment   The object described and sketched by Hugh Rowand is the same as the one that appears in the film, as shown by the enlargement obtained from a still (see plate 11 and hold at arm's length)—but as I had never read or heard of anyone referring to it as a 'fin-like' object before, I questioned this point in a subsequent letter and this is the reply I got—

My use of the word 'fin-like' was meant to convey something rather like this—(see sketch). It is a moot point whether one would say such an object was a fin or a hump, and I presume, depends on the degree of radius at the apex.

This is of course fair comment, and that is why I have included it. It is important that people say exactly what they think about the Monster and that they make their own comparisons, because there is a risk of repeating other people's neat phrases and descriptive terms too easily. However, it is necessary to accentuate the fact that Hugh Rowand did not actually say it *was* a fin, but that the object appeared 'fin-like'. Actually, it is definitely not a fin, because I examined it carefully through binoculars before filming, and the object has width—4 or 5 ft of width, when viewed from the rear.

Account no. 2a

Witness: Mr H. L. Cockrell, professional trout farmer, Dumfries. 59 years of age.
Date of occurrence: autumn of 1958.

As a result of correspondence between us Mr Cockrell (who is a serious student of the Monster), sent me the series of articles he wrote for the *Weekly Scotsman* newspaper, in 1958. They outline the course of his studies and opinions, and describe his remarkable experience with the Monster—or what certainly appeared to be a very large swimming animal, which he met at close quarters in a canoe, on the waters of Loch Ness. Mr Cockrell, who is an expert seaman and is familiar with small craft of all kinds, has developed a waterproofed camera with flash equipment which he used with effect from his kayak. The camera is carried on his head, rather like the lamp on a miner's hat, and is triggered by the action of his mouth, thus leaving his hands free to handle the paddle.

After two unsuccessful all-night hunts on the eerie dangerous waters of the loch, Mr Cockrell made a third and last attempt, determined to conquer the very natural uneasiness that crept upon him as he slid over the glassy waters with every star a reflecting pinprick of light, and every shadow a potential threat—and then, at first light, this is what he described:

Just about dawn I had my first real test. A light breeze suddenly dropped and left me on a mirror surface about half way between shores, with Invermoriston almost abeam to starboard. Something appeared—or I noticed it for the first time—about 50 yards away on my port bow. It seemed to be swimming very steadily and converging on me. It looked like a very large flat head four or five feet long, and wide. About three feet astern of this I noticed another thin line. All very low in the water; just awash.

I was convinced it was the head and back of a very large creature. It looked slightly whiskery and misshapen. I simply could not believe it. I was not a bit amused. With a considerable effort of will I swung to intercept, and to my horror it appeared to shear towards me with ponderous power.

I hesitated. There was no one near on that great sheet of water to witness a retreat, but it was obviously too late to run. Curiously enough I found this a great relief. My heart began to beat normally and my muscles suddenly felt in good trim. I took a shot with my camera in case I got too close for my focus—and went in. The creature headed slightly away, and my morale revived completely. I had another shot and closed in to pass along it, as I didn't want to be thrown into the air with a rising hump or two.

There was a slight squall out of the glen behind Invermoriston, and the object appeared to sink. When the squall cleared I could see something on the surface. I closed in again cautiously; it remained motionless and I found it was a long stick about an inch thick. I thankfully assumed it to be my Monster and took it aboard as a souvenir. Suddenly I felt very tired and stiff and wanted my breakfast . . .

Mr Cockrell then returned home, but when the film was developed and printed: 'The film showed things I had not noticed either through fatigue of the night or—let's face it—the fright of the dawn. The film showed quite a large affair which had a distinct wash. There was no reason for this wash because the picture shows the water to be mirror calm, a fact clearly demonstrated by the reflection of the hills.

What caused the wash? Could it have been Nessie after all? I just don't know.

Another point: the creature was seen by a Mr Brown and his wife from Invergordon next day, in the same place but further inshore. He describes it as 'three big black humps, churning through the water leaving a foaming trail, with 30 yards ahead of the humps a curious wake on the surface which seemed to be the leading part, or the head.' Mr Brown and I have never met and at the time no one knew of my own experience.

Comment The photograph obtained is reproduced on plate 2 and shows a part of the shore of the loch which is clearly recognizable to those who are familiar with the place, and in addition, a very interesting shape in the water, producing what appears to be a distinct wash—to the *left* of each solid object only; suggesting that if there was movement, it must have been towards the right.

It is clear from this account that Mr Cockrell deserves full marks for ingenuity and courage—although in my own opinion I believe he may have been running a greater risk than he appreciated at the time of his experience.

Account no. 2b

Witness: self.
Date of occurrence: 23 April 1960.

It is only necessary to record a few pertinent facts about the film, under this heading.
Camera used: Paillard Bolex 16-mm. with 135-mm. lens.
Film speed: 24 frames per second.
Aperture: f 11.
Film: Kodak Plus X. Rated, 50 A.S.A.
Range: 1,600 yards increasing to 1,800 yards.
Time of day: 9 a.m.
The boat in the film had a length of 15 ft, beam of 5 ft., freeboard of 2 ft. and was propelled at full throttle at 7 m.p.h. by a 5 h.p. outboard.

Comment   There is little I need add to what has already been recorded except to say that the back of the animal I saw so clearly through binoculars was unlike anything I have seen before; and I have watched the following creatures disport themselves on the surface of the sea, lakes or rivers at one time or another: whales, of various types, big and little; basking sharks, and the other more common varieties; dolphins, porpoises, seals, crocodiles; and a giant sturgeon in the mouth of the Ottawa river. To my certain knowledge, none of these animals bear any resemblance to the back of the animal filmed in Loch Ness.

I am prepared to take an oath to the effect that the film is genuine and untouched, and that it portrays the back and wash of a large living creature of some variety unknown to me, and that I did examine it carefully through a pair of excellent Carl Heinrich 7 × 16 binoculars (which were quite adequate) before deciding to film.

All this seems rather unnecessary, but for the fact that statements have recently been published suggesting that the object in the film is something quite ordinary, or just another boat! This is manifestly absurd, because the film demonstrates that the object— whatever it is—travels first on the surface at the speed of a motor boat but without leaving a propeller wash, and then dives beneath the surface and proceeds for half a mile, at approximately ten knots, leaving a much greater wash without any visible sign of the cause of disturbance.

Account no. 2c

The Universities (Oxford and Cambridge) Expedition.
Dates: 27 June–23 July 1960.

Purpose: To make a general study of Loch Ness, its geology and ecology—'paying particular attention to the possible existence of the so called Loch Ness Monster'.
Numbers: About thirty graduates and undergraduates voluntarily took part.
Equipment: Cameras and echo sounder apparatus, mounted on a boat.
Results: One clear sighting of what appeared to be the Monster's back moving through the water. One indeterminate lengthy sighting of an object that continuously changed shape on the surface. Several echo soundings of unusual character.

Comment   This expedition was, without doubt, the first scientifically planned venture of its kind to visit the loch, and was prompted by a lecture given in the spring of 1960 by Dr Denys Tucker, who was much interested in this strange phenomenon. Dr Tucker made a case for the need to investigate, and students from both universities took him up on it. They worked hard, but were hampered by bad weather and lack of sufficient equipment and the results, though intriguing, were not conclusive. The work and findings of this expedition was subsequently written up in the *Scotsman* newspaper on 12, 13 and 14 September 1960.

Account no. 2d—from a letter dated 21 August 1960.
Witness: Mr Torquil MacLeod.
Date of occurrence: 7 August 1960.

You will be interested to know that two Sundays ago my wife, myself, the Smiths (whom you met) and the crew of a small yacht all saw the Loch Ness Monster for about 20 minutes—time approx. 4.40 p.m. The details follow below.
Weather: First calm, dry day for some time, warm rather than hot. Humid. Visibility good to excellent. 'Catspaws' on loch surface.

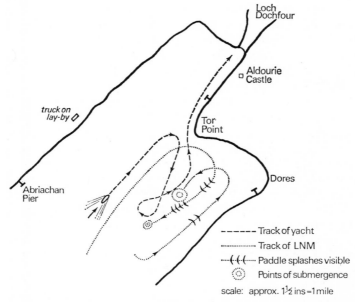

Figure 16   Sketch drawn by Torquil MacLeod of his sighting, 7 August 1960.

Date time: 4.40 p.m. Sunday, 7 August 1960.

Locality: Off Tor point, to near Dores and adjacent beaches.

Range: 1,600 to 2,100 yards, checked against 1 in. to 1 mile ordnance survey map.

Binoculars: Ross 7 × 50 also 5 × Goertz.

Observed speeds: The L.N.M. 8–9 knots. The yacht, $5\frac{1}{2}$–$6\frac{1}{2}$ knots (authority for this later obtained from owner. These speeds correct certainly to within 10%).

Position from which observed: Motor lay-by 7–8 miles N.E. of Abriachan pier. i.e. almost opposite Dores village.

Characteristics: First—wash only. Second—one hump, approx. 10 ft. × few inches high. Third—hump, plus *two pairs* of paddle splashes similar to a swimmer using a 'butterfly' stroke, paddles not actually seen, but separate pairs quite clear. Rear splashes *twice* the size of front ones. Fourth—wash only ending in abrupt submergence.

Remarks: I was driving S.W. along the main road towards Abriachan pier when I noticed a small yacht motoring up the loch. Suddenly I realized there were *two* V wakes, parallel to one another. The nearest came from the yacht and about 200 yards further on the second appeared to be caused by something just submerged. Second wake overhauled yacht, which turned towards it. L.N.M.'s wake turned in wide sweep towards Dores, and took reciprocal course, without increasing speed noticeably.

Yacht turned more sharply and converged on L.N.M. which then submerged for a few moments reappearing on a course parallel to its original one, only by now about 400 yards off Dores. Yacht turned again, so did L.N.M. which then submerged again—maintaining a horizontal trim, as a basking shark does. It looked just like a midget sub minus its periscope (I have seen M subs awash quite often). The yacht owner, who isn't willing 'to get involved' subsequently told me that he approached to about 150 ft. and considered that to be close enough as he had young children on board. He described the shape as 'vague', no definite signs of paddles, neck, tail fins or anything. The colour was 'greenish black', the size 'about the size of the boat'—which was in fact 48 × 10 ft.!

The owner got some snaps, but the angle plus the refraction will probably spoil them because he could see nothing definite with the naked eye.

In conclusion, it (the wake) looked exactly as it did in your film, when it was splashing.

Comment   I have included this report because I know and respect the man who made it, and because it is such a good example of how a report on this subject *should* be prepared and laid out. It is also very interesting, particularly the part about the two pairs of paddle splashes, with the greater at the rear. Actually, the observer has since told me these splashes reached to a height of 4 ft. or so above the water. The size of the animal is remarkable, and I believe indicates that there is one, at least, truly enormous animal in the loch. There is much evidence to support this view, of which more later.

Account no. 2e

Witness: The Reverend W. L. Dobb, Wimborne, Dorset.
Date of occurrence: 13 August 1960.

This account was reported briefly in the press, and as a result of subsequent correspondence, Rev. Dobb kindly agreed to let me publish his account exactly as it appeared in the September issue of the St Michael Colehill parish magazine.

Most of us are sceptical about something at sometime or another, and I am no exception. One object of my scepticism has been the Loch Ness Monster. I have dared to entertain ideas that the Monster had something to do with the fertile imagination of someone concerned with the tourist business, and I have even had the unforgiveable thought that this particular 'Monster' had the same origin as another Monster—the proverbial 'pink elephant'! Shame on me for entertaining such ideas, for from 3.15 p.m. on Saturday August 13th, no such thoughts will ever enter my head and I am a sceptic no longer. At that time, on that date, we all of us (my wife, Timothy, Christopher and I) saw quite unexpectedly something which convinced us that there is a living creature in Loch Ness, which is quite abnormal.

We had had lunch at a site overlooking the loch, which was then so calm it looked like a sheet of blue glass. We joked about the Monster, and were then as sceptical as ever, and, for the sake of what follows, may I explain our only beverage was tea! The meal over, we hitched up the caravan again and set off for the last lap of the journey to Portsoy. We had gone only about three miles when a car in front of us pulled up very suddenly almost in the middle of the road, and its driver, regardless of what might be behind him, got out and rushed to the loch side of the road. I pulled up as suddenly and looked to see what had caused this action of the driver in front. And there was the phenomenon which shattered all our sceptical jokes. Large waves (not just ripples) arrow-shaped, were moving along the water, just as if a motor boat was ploughing through the loch, but no boat was to be seen. A few seconds later, to the great delight of the children, and to the amazement of my wife and myself, a large black 'hump' appeared in the middle of the waves, only to disappear again as quickly as it had appeared. But very shortly afterwards, as the waves continued to travel away from us, *two* 'humps' appeared and remained visible for several seconds. It was quite obvious that something very large was travelling through the water quite near the surface, though apart from the waves it was making, we saw nothing further, and, in an atmosphere of excitement, we continued our journey.

Comment   This is of course an excellent testimonial in every respect, and there are several points worth mentioning. Firstly, Rev. Dobb was not a believer, he had never seen the film, or read either of the two books on the subject, and yet his description of the wake might be taken from the soundtrack I dubbed onto my film—with one exception: the two humps. This is important because it demonstrates that one hump can very quickly develop into a two, suggesting that the humps really are part of the basic structure of the beast.

3   New evidence of the Monster on shore

Account no. 3a—from a letter dated 19 September 1960.
Witness: Mr Torquil MacLeod.
Date of occurrence: 28 February 1960.

Because of the importance of this account, it is necessary to introduce it with a few brief words; it is from the same individual who provided the information for report no. 2d, in such an excellent manner. I have included his statement and sketches, which have been very carefully copied from the original, because Torquil MacLeod was both a full-time investigator at Loch Ness, and a trained artist.

At approximately 3.30–3.45 p.m. on February 28th, 1960, I was driving towards Fort Augustus from Invermoriston and, when approximately $2\frac{1}{2}$ miles *from* Invermoriston, I had occasion to pull up, and my attention was attracted by a slight movement upon the opposite shore (there is no road along this 8 mile stretch). The weather was dull and overcast, with a drizzle drifting down the loch. The wind was W.N.W. Force 1 to 2, Temperature about 50 degrees Fahrenheit. Humid.

Upon turning my glasses on the moving object, I saw a large grey black mass (I am inclined to think the skin was wet and dry in patches) and at the front there was what looked like an outsize in elephants' trunks. Paddles were visible on both sides, but only at what I presumed was the rear end, and it was this end (remote from the 'trunk'), which tapered off into the water. The animal was on a steep slope, and taking its backbone as an approximate straight line, was inclined about 15–20 degrees out of my line of sight: the 'trunk' being at the top and to the left, and the tail at the bottom, in the water, to the right.

I was able to pinpoint both my own and the animal's position on the 1 in. ordnance map (1 inch to the mile), the distance being approximately 1,700 yards—to within 50 yards. The animal was near a burn marked on the map, and I was only yards away from a house which was also marked—hence the accurate pinpoint.

For about 8 or 9 minutes the animal remained quite still, but for its 'trunk' (I assume neck, although I could not recognize a head as such) which occasionally moved from side to side with a slight up and down motion—just like a snake about to strike; but quite slowly. It was, to my mind, obviously scanning the shores of the loch in each direction.

In the end it made a sort of half jump—half lurch to the left, its 'trunk' coming right round until it was facing me, then it flopped into the water and apparently went straight down; so it must be very deep close inshore at that point.* As it turned I saw distinctly a large squarish ended flipper *forward* of the big rear paddles—or flippers: call them what you will, but *not* legs. I did not see the end of the tail at any time, but the animal looked something like this . . . (here the sketches were included).

My glasses are Ross 7 × 50 and have graticulations—degrees and minutes of arc as hairlines, and I looked up the Almanac tables and was able to establish the animal's length at approximately 45 ft., but allowing for the *angle off* this makes it at least 51 ft., possibly 55 ft. or so in length—*the visible parts only, remember*. I have no idea of the proportionate length of its tail and its neck, but I suspect it is shorter and wider.

That's about all I can tell you and conditions were by no means ideal. I think the L.N.M. looks like this . . .

Comment What comment can one make that is adequate ? There is little that can or need be said, and not surprisingly perhaps the observer (who was known to me as a friend) felt much the same way about it after his experience.

For several hours afterwards he remained very much subdued,

---

* Actually it is; the wall of the loch underwater is almost vertical.

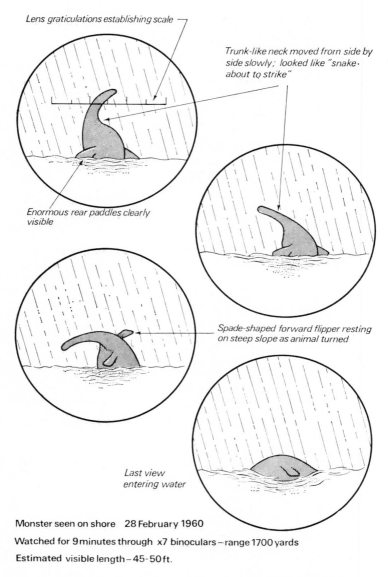

Lens graticulations establishing scale

Trunk-like neck moved from side by side slowly; looked like "snake-about to strike"

Enormous rear paddles clearly visible

Spade-shaped forward flipper resting on steep slope as animal turned

Last view entering water

Monster seen on shore 28 February 1960

Watched for 9 minutes through x7 binoculars – range 1700 yards

Estimated visible length – 45-50 ft.

Figure 17 Sketch drawn by Torquil MacLeod of his sighting, 28 February 1960.

"I think the LNM looks like this ···"

Figure 18   Torquil MacLeod's impression of the Monster.

and it may be that in viewing the creature out of water, though not the first to enjoy this experience, he was the first man to appreciate its staggering significance, because the Monster was a subject about which he spoke with authority and knowledge.

Viewing the incident with purely clinical interest however, there are one or two points which must be mentioned. Once more the head is not distinguishable, by virtue of its smallness, and once again the stupendous size of the beast is brought into focus. It is this evidence of size which confirms my own belief that there is one creature in Loch Ness which is of gargantuan proportions— the old bull of the tribe perhaps. There are a dozen or so perfectly clear reports suggesting the presence of one huge, whole animal of quite these proportions—not two or three little ones, swimming in a row, as is sometimes suggested. This creature is I believe the 'water bull' to which reference is made in ancient Gaelic legend, and which has put the fear of death into so many different people.

Report no. 3b—from a letter dated 9 January 1961.

Witness: Alfred Cruickshank, Buckie, Banffshire.

Date of occurrence: April 1923.

The following account of a 'Monster' on shore has not been published before, to my knowledge, and is certainly the earliest recorded of this particular phenomenon—

> I thank you for your letter about our famous 'Nessie'. I
> usually went from Buckie to Speanbridge to meet a train
> from Glasgow at 8 a.m. This meant leaving home about
> 3 a.m. as the roads at this time were very narrow and rough,
> 112 miles. The car I had was a Model T Ford and the

headlamps were off the low tension magneto. The faster your engine ran the better the lights, so that when you slowed down at a corner (there were hundreds of them) your lamps faded. I have done this journey hundreds of times but I have had only one view of the Monster, and I believe I was the first to see it, but I never told anybody (bar my wife) what I had seen (also my boss). If I remember rightly it was on a Monday morning in April, 1923, when I was going to Speanbridge, that I had the encounter with the Monster, of which I got a very good view as it crossed the road in front of me; but as I was nearing a corner of the road I was slowing up and the headlamps dimmed. I can still show you the place although the road has all been remade and widened. If the road had been wider I would have turned the car for a further look but it was too narrow. My view of the Monster was: Body 10–12 ft. long, 5ft 6in.–7 ft. in height, tail 10–12 ft. Colour, green-khaki resembling a frog, with cream coloured belly which, trailed on the ground. It had four legs thick like an elephant's and had large webbed feet, in reality it looked like an enormous hippo, but arched back and long trailing tail which was on the same level as the belly, as you will see in my rough drawing. It gave out a sharp bark, like a dog, as it disappeared over the road into the water.

I think this is all the information I can give you. I wrote the B.B.C. about the Monster when they put down divers to photograph under Loch Ness for the Monster, for one bite of its large mouth would have halved any man, but they never replied. Hoping I have been of some assistance to you . . .

Comment I am indebted to Mr Cruickshank for his sincere and interesting letter, which I have studied carefully, together with his outline drawing. Although both his account and the sketch differ in some respects from the usual run of Monster reports, in others they are similar. To my mind the most interesting feature of the account is that Mr Cruickshank refers to this huge and extraordinary animal on the shores of Loch Ness approximately *ten years* before anyone but the local people knew it existed; and the fact that he saw it by the fading lights of his Model T Ford, for a few moments only, may help to explain the parts of the report which seem to be at variance with the established Monster specification.

Account no. 3c
Witness: self.
Date of occurrence: July 1960.

Under this heading it is necessary to refer to a rather curious item of 'evidence'—which has as much right to the term as any other that comes from the shores of the loch; though whether it is valid or not is a matter for the reader to decide. On the second expedition to the loch, I got to hear of the 'Monster's Claw', which was kept in a house near Drumnadrochit. It was, I was told, the foot of some strange creature and had enormous talons on it. Overcome with curiosity I managed to track it down, and thanks to the kindness of the lady of the house was allowed to photograph it. As a matter of fact my colour pictures did not come out well, but a friend has since sent me a copy of his own picture which shows it clearly. At first sight I was surprised at the huge size of the foot and its beautiful state of preservation. It measured some 13 inches by 7, and had been found on the shore near Urquhart Castle a short distance away. Though I am not an expert in zoology it looked to me like the trophy foot of a huge crocodile, and I was inclined to dismiss it. Further investigation has since introduced an intriguing possibility, though it has almost certainly confirmed the fact it *is* a hinder foot from a very large crocodile, perhaps of the Indian 'gharial' type, which it resembles closely.

Years ago it is reported by Gould that a retired South African took a small croft between Dores and Foyers. Because he had developed a liking for crocodiles when in Africa he wrote to a friend in that country and got him to send three young specimens, which he subsequently kept in a tank. As the crocodiles grew bigger, the man became afraid of them and made arrangements to send them to a zoo, but while the correspondence was still in progress one of the crocodiles disappeared. As it was never found it was thought to have made its way into the loch—where, as Gould suggests, it probably died of the cold, although it is *just possible* that it might have become acclimatized and grown to a great size, and hoary old age. The curious thing about this whole business is that Gould postulates in a later analysis that the long thin snout of the Indian Gangetic gavial or gharial crocodile might conceivably be mistaken for a long thin neck sticking up out of the water—and unless I am mistaken, this really does look like the foot of a gharial, and a very big one at that!

However, all things considered I have not the least doubt that it is a hunter's trophy and not the foot of the Monster. There are three factors involved, which establish this to be the case. First, the foot is enormous; and most hunters' trophies are from large or record-breaking animals. Secondly, it is in such beautiful condition—it would be a prize in any museum. Thirdly, it was found on the one, if not the only part of the shore of the loch where visitors constantly visit—that near Urquhart Castle! But there is always the possibility I may be wrong on all three counts and that it is in fact the 'Monster's Claw', because on 7 June 1933 in the newspaper *Argus* the following statement appeared.
'Sir, having seen in the local press the report of a strange monster in Loch Ness, it might interest you to learn that while flying over that loch last week in the vicinity of Urquhart Castle we beheld in the depths a shape resembling a large alligator, the size of which would be about 25 ft. long by 4 ft. wide.'

4 Monster population evidence

Accounts of more than one animal seen in the loch at the same moment are by no means rare, though they are *unusual* and they are of course of prime importance. It is only from these reports that any idea of possible numbers can be gained; though it is to be hoped that in the near future modern echo sounding equipment will provide an accurate means of deciding the existing population, on a far more accurate basis.

In her book Mrs Whyte refers to at least five reports in which people have seen two creatures on the surface at the same time, and I know that Alex Campbell, in the early 1930s, saw two separate animals and a third disturbance in the water on one occasion. There is also the fascinating account of what may have been baby Monsters* seen by two schoolboys from a boat near Fort Augustus, in June 1937. Their stories were checked independently by one of the monks from the Abbey, Dom Cyril Dieckhoff, who found they agreed in every detail. The boys claimed to have seen three small lizard-like creatures swimming away from the wash of the boat. About three feet in length, they were rather like eels but had definite necks and four rudimentary limbs. The fore pair were flipperlike and did not seem to be used as a primary source of propulsion, whereas the hind pair were

* *More Than a Legend*, p. 83.

held close to the body and used for pushing—or so it appeared. They were dark grey in colour.

The following report in which *three* Monsters were seen on the surface at the same time is nearly twenty-four years old. Although the purpose of this section is really to record recent 'multiple' reports, which are the only ones of value in estimating numbers today, I have recorded it, because it is of such unique interest. I was sent the report by Father J. A. Carruth at the Abbey, to whom one of the witnesses, Robert R. Gourlay, wrote personally. The *Daily Express* account dated 14 July 1937 reads as follows:

The appearance of three monsters was reported to the *Scottish Daily Express* at Inverness yesterday. The Monsters were seen by eight people, including Mr and Mrs A. Stevenson of Brackla, their two daughters and four holiday visitors; Mrs R. R. Gourlay, Ireland; Mr R. R. Gourlay, Jun., and his wife, and Mrs. S. J. Stevenson of Bristol.

The party were at breakfast yesterday when Mrs Gourlay, jun. drew attention to the loch through the open window. They all ran to the door from where they saw what appeared to be three Monsters about 300 yards out in the loch. In the centre were two black shiny humps, 5 ft. long and protruding 2 ft. out of the water and on either side was a smaller Monster, one of which made a great splashing noise as it disappeared towards the opposite shore. The largest Monster and the other smaller ones then travelled together in the direction of Urquhart Castle.

The party states the surface of the loch was disturbed for some time after the Monsters, which they had watched for five minutes, disappeared.

Account no. 4b—from a letter dated 18 August 1960.

Witness: Mr D. Campbell, headmaster, Dores School.
Date of occurrence: 16 June 1957.

The following account comes from a responsible person who has been most helpful in providing reports and information of one kind or another.

Apart from the usual sightings a good many people have told me that while looking down on the loch from above they have seen what appeared to be a rowing boat, which a few seconds later disappeared below the surface in a flash. This is more or less all that I ever saw of the 'Monster', although you will understand I have scanned the surface on innumerable occasions in the hope of seeing something. It was on a Sunday several years ago. I was sitting on a hillside above the loch and I was reading. I happened to glance down at the water and saw what I was quite satisfied were two rowing boats, about half a mile west of Dores village and a quarter mile from the shore. They appeared to have outboard motors and were travelling in the direction of Urquhart Castle, on a parallel course, and at least 150 yards apart. There was nothing particularly remarkable seeing two boats there except that it was unusual for rowing boats even with outboard engines to travel in that direction, and at that distance from the shore. I would say that my view point was over a mile away. After a few moments I was about to return to my book, when the 'boat' on the left suddenly moved at right angles, and in a flash passed behind the 'boat' to the right, and then both of them just disappeared!

When I got home I spoke of what I had seen, and remarked that if it was the Monster someone else would be sure to have seen it. Sure enough the next day the Monster was reported as having been seen near Urquhart Castle at almost the same time of day.

I am reporting what I saw as objectively as possible as I am still not committed to the popular conception of the size or shape or even the fact that there is a large underwater creature of unknown species. I must admit, however, that apart from the tentative theory I already gave I have no alternative explanation of the phenomenon which is so often recorded by credible witnesses.

Comment   Mr Campbell's theory is perfectly legitimate and refers to the possibility that currents in Loch Ness may, from time to time, throw up objects like waterlogged tree trunks or other flotsam. This may be the case; though it cannot really explain the evidence.

9 Entrenchments of doubt

In July 1960 I went back to Loch Ness for a period of nine days, but did not see the 'Beastie' again. This is the name by which it was known to some of the local people; it carried with it a flavour of superstition from centuries past. I came to rather like the term, in contradistinction to 'Monster', though the latter, I knew, would remain the common and more descriptive title.

By now I had become so much engrossed in the study of the phenomena, particularly with regard to species and possible origin, that I had less and less time for my ordinary work. Inevitably a decision had to be made whether or not I should continue with a career in aeronautics.

In March 1961 I spent ten icy days motoring round the loch, sleeping in my car and probing the more lonely and inaccessible places. I had too much equipment—a giant 36-inch lens mounted on a tripod to which was affixed a 16-mm camera; and a 300-mm lens, and various other cameras. I had too little weatherproof clothing, and nearly froze as a result. It taught me a lesson. In future I would operate only the minimum and best photo equipment, and practise the art of keeping dry and warm.

In May I went back to the loch again, unable to resist the compulsive attraction it held for me—and endured the effects of sunburn instead, caused by working out of doors in an unexpected heatwave. By now it was clear that almost any type of weather could be met at the loch, at any time of year, and in it one had to remain effectively on watch for ten or fifteen hours. But the extraordinary natural beauties of the place, and the occasional contortion of excitement made up for the discomforts.

Back in England, later in the summer, I met a man who was to play a major role at Loch Ness: David James, M.B.E., D.S.C., a Member of Parliament, wartime naval officer, author, Antarctic traveller. He brought with him the promise of support—and a welcome touch of humour. A Highlander, he understood the problems posed by the Monster. Before long he helped to found the Loch Ness Investigation Bureau (LNIB), a non-profit making company. Its main objective was to rally support, collect evidence,

I

and help to sponsor fieldwork. As preparations take time it was 1962 before the first Bureau expedition set up its equipment.

The need for some such organization was obvious. In 1961 arrangements were made for a meeting of senior zoologists to examine the case as it then stood. I attended this meeting with several other witnesses, including Torquil MacLeod, the man who had seen the Monster out of water in February the year before (see rep. 3a). He had seen it again, in company with Lis, his Australian wife and co-researcher, when it surfaced close to a yacht in August of that year (see rep. 2d). The owner and skipper of the yacht *Finola*, Mr Lowrie, was in attendance too, together with his family who were all witnesses to the event. He also brought a photograph taken from the deck, showing the Monster's wake on glassy water, at a range of just a few yards. The creature was so large that 'a hurried family conference unanimously decided something sinister was approaching, and that we should alter course to avoid close contact.'

These comments, my own film, which was clear enough, and MacLeod's corroborating evidence made a case no one could really doubt—but again without any noticeable effect.

The results, or lack of results, of this meeting convinced me of the futility of argument, and the vital need to continue working at Loch Ness to obtain close-up ciné film. Besides there was a principle at stake. But to do more than simply talk about it would mean an end to aeronautics, and the income that stemmed from it. At thirty-eight, with a family of four, I could see no alternative.

One did materialize, however. Until 1968 I was virtually in private business, which gave me time to make expeditions, and travel in response to invitations to lecture on the subject.

During this period, which was difficult financially, a great deal happened; it is only possible to itemize the main events. Subsequently, I was able to become a full-time 'monster hunter'—a serious occupation, which must rank as one of the most extraordinary on record, but in the human sense, it is perhaps one of the most rewarding.

In 1960 a zenith had been reached, in terms of photography and sightings, with two still pictures taken at close range, a 16-mm film, and the corroborated Lowrie sighting. Torquil MacLeod had seen the Beastie on land too, though one had to take his word for this. But his reports were reliable. I had proof of this—because when he first told me about his observation of the yacht *Finola* (which account I published), no one knew where Mr Lowrie and his family had gone. Once out of the Caledonian Canal they simply disappeared to seaward. It was not until 1961 that I found he had been traced, and he supported Torquil's story.

In 1961, however, no progress was in evidence, and officialdom continued to ignore the facts. To be truthful, I no longer cared very much. If people were, for some reason best known to themselves, unwilling to take the initiative and to do so openly I felt we were better off without them; and there was every sign that private expeditions would again be active in 1962. Students from Cambridge were planning to try again. Colonel Hasler, of 'Cockleshell Heroes' fame, and founder of the trans-Atlantic single-handed yachtsman's race, intended to put his junk-rigged yacht *Jester* on Loch Ness, and keep a 24-hour watch over a period of two months, changing crews repeatedly. David James had ideas as well, and inevitably my own plans were developing.

In the event all these expeditions went into the field, starting a tradition of voluntary work which was to continue throughout the next decade.

Before the end of 1961, however, something happened which helped me to make my chilling personal decision. After two years of full-time, privately sponsored investigation at Loch Ness, Torquil MacLeod died. He and Lis had been working from a croft-house high up in the mountains.

I had met Torquil through Mrs Constance Whyte the year before, and had listened intently to his account of seeing the Beastie on land in February 1960. Torquil and I had enjoyed a sense of brotherhood. On the two occasions we had watched together, I had found in him a radiating quality of spirit, undiminished by the rare disease which was killing him, a type of blood cancer. He had lived longer than expected, and died doing what he wanted to do most—researching the mystery; a marvellous ending to his extraordinary, adventurous life, the story of which would make a book in itself.

In the spring and autumn of 1962 I made two more expeditions without seeing anything of note, but I was learning, and had graduated from amateur to professional ciné equipment, with variable focus lens, and sound recording as an added tool.

Commencing in June Colonel H. G. Hasler, D.S.O., O.B.E., brought *Jester* in through the Caledonian Canal; for two months he watched the surface, and listened through hydrophones for underwater noises. Fifty-six volunteers worked with him. In early

July the Cambridge undergraduate's expedition mounted shore cameras, and did more extensive work with fish-finding sonars, under the leadership of two scientific graduates, Mark Westwood and Peter Baker.

The *Observer* newspaper reported both these undertaking: Hasler's on 3 June and 19 August, and Baker and Westwood's on 26 August. Possible sightings of hump, back, and neck, some hydrophone noises and curious echo tracings made up the bag of unexplained phenomena—but again, there was nothing conclusive.

In mid-October David James—or D.J. as he was coming to be known—and a merry company of twenty-six enthusiasts joined in with a pair of army searchlights, hoping to 'shoot' the Monster down the beam at night; but the Beastie did not condescend to show itself during the hours of darkness. It did, however, give itself away in daylight—a dark shape swimming just under the surface contrary to wind and ripple; in front of it salmon were seen to leap. The episode was recorded on 35 mm. black and white film, which was shown on television, and then submitted to a panel of four scientists, with a special knowledge of marine biology, wild-life photography, and the behaviour of otters. In due course they reported on their work, stating clearly that 'We find there is some unidentified animate object in Loch Ness, which, if it be a mammal, amphibian, reptile, fish or mollusc of any known order, is of such a size as to be worthy of careful scientific examination and identification'.

Unfortunately this conclusion did not cause any particular stir, or any change in the official attitude. In 1963 efforts were again voluntary, though supported by money from ATV, who were impressed by these results.

The LNIB manned another two-week expedition, watching in daylight with long range 35 mm. cameras. Film was exposed on two occasions when objects were seen on the surface, and once when a curious oily slick appeared. Pictorially, the films were unimpressive; one was spoiled by a heavy mist (or 'haar', to give it a local name), and the other by mere distance. In both, however analysis suggested a large object; one apparently emerging from the fringe water of the loch near a shingle beach. The slick might well have been excreta (for example, seals excrete an oily liquid after a meal of herring), but there was no boat at hand with which to gain a sample.

In 1963 and 1964 I worked from a lonely 'hide' on the southern shore of the loch, making two more private expeditions, but with no luck whatsoever. Indeed my luck seemed to have deserted me. On one trip I had pneumonia, and on the other I fell down an almost precipitous slope, and thought I had broken my back—but the ominous crack had come from a shattered movie camera, which had landed under me.

By now I had watched for more than 700 hours, and was beginning to appreciate the good fortune which had put the Monster squarely in my sights in less than one tenth of that time—but there was, of course, no question of giving up. More and more interested people were beginning to join the hunt. Some worked on their own and others collectively, but most took part in the LNIB expeditions which worked from the northern shore with its motor road, and better communications.

One of these people was Mr F. W. (Ted) Holiday, the well-known fishing writer. He had an expansive mind, and the courage to express himself. In 1963 he obtained a most unusual and exciting tape-recording from two local men who had been fishing for trout off Tor point. On a late evening in July, in calm water, they saw the head and neck of the Monster rear out of the loch 20–30 yards from them. It was alive and powerful. The neck was about 1 ft in diameter. Both men were shaken, but did not panic. It submerged vertically downwards. In his report to the LNIB the following comments appear, 'The head was held at a slight angle to the neck. Mr MacI. said the head reminded him of a bulldog, i.e. flat on top with a powerful lower face. He saw no eyes or tentacles. Colour of head and neck was blackish brown. The head was wide and extremely ugly. Part of a hump was also visible . . . the neck was fringed by what looked like coarse black hair.'

In a letter to me later Holiday said 'Had a curious impression when questioning . . . I couldn't put it in my report. When people are confronted by this fantastic animal at close quarters they seem to be stunned. There is something strange about Nessie that has nothing to do with size and appearance. . . . Odd, isn't it?'

The fisherman had also told him, 'There is certainly a weird beastie in the loch'; and that he didn't expect anyone to believe in the Monster until they had seen it with their own eyes.

After first showing at very close range, then descending vertically like a periscope, the neck had broken surface twice more at greater distance. Both men allowed their names to be used in the report, but otherwise wished to remain anonymous. From then on Ted Holiday began to collect taped accounts of sightings.

This is probably the best way of recording verbal evidence because of the inflections, accents and reactions to questioning, which together combine to produce a sound-picture, or catalogue, of events which is unique.

In 1964 the LNIB mounted its first summer-long expedition. With the help of technicians from ATV, two magnificent long-range photo rigs were built. Mounted on Moy gear-traversing heads, they carried a 35 mm. ciné camera with 1000-ft magazine, and 36-inch lens; and two big F24 motorized aircraft still-cameras on cantilever arms, toed in to provide stereoscopic cover. Actuated at 12-second intervals by a timer, the whole apparatus was aimed through a telescope and triggered by a single switch.

Based on the previous year's results over two weeks, there were few who thought the Monster would escape entirely, and yet between May and August no photography was obtained, in spite of several good reports of sightings from other parts of the loch. Two camera sites had been chosen, almost facing each other on opposite sides of the water. The headquarters were at the shingle beach to the south, at the place where the colour film in 1963 showed an object in the shallows—an idyllic spot. From the battlements at Urquhart Castle a platform extended out over the loch, built from scaffolding. It was a dramatic point for observation.

In August Sandy Bay was shut down, and the watch continued from Urquhart with diminished crews. I volunteered to do a final stint as group-commander, during the first two weeks of October. With only five people, ranging in age from forty to almost seventy, we worked continuously. Two and sometimes three camera sites were maintained giving full cover of Urquhart Bay, interlinked by field telephone. The weather was good, and the autumn colours magnificent. I also watched huge numbers of migrating salmon making their sure way back to the spawning beds of the rivers Oich and Tarff, and Moriston, further to the west—a sight which would not be repeated, because of the lethal game-fish virus, and the stupid commercial depredations of the Greenland fishing banks.

But the expedition was defeated and no pictures were obtained. David James wrote a report for the *Observer* newspaper, which had contributed £1,000. Entitled 'Fine Weather Monster' it was published on 27 December 1964, and gave a clear account of the year's activities, sightings, and researches. It also included references to comparable monster sightings from other places: a 30–40 ft humped object seen at 300–400 yards in Loch Morar; a head and neck in the sea-loch Linnhe, entrance to Great Glen fault; a large humped back in Loch Lomond; and a huge long-necked creature seen (and later sketched) standing partly out of water at Lake Khaiyr, in north-east Siberia!

In 1965 David James organized the north-shore activities, which ran for 150 days. The new headquarters were at Achnahannet, a field some 200 ft above the loch slightly west of Urquhart Bay, with a sweeping view of the water. Sandy Bay, and the Castle site were not used. Instead vehicles took camera crews out to likely places during flat-calm conditions, when the record showed 95 per cent of reported sightings occurred. Altogether 1,736 hours of watching were logged from Achnahannet, and some 500 more put in by the mobile units. The weather was atrocious, with only 44 hours logged when it was both calm and sunny. Torrents of rain fell all summer; in late July when I ran a team for this expedition, the loch was brim full, spilling out over Telford's weir in a cascade several feet in depth.

On 30 July the *Aberdeen Press and Journal* reported that two businessmen had watched a very large humped animal swimming down the river Ness towards the sea, when standing on the step of the YMCA hall in Inverness! Mr Hamish Ferguson, of Gullane, East Lothian, told the newspaper 'This has absolutely amazed me. It was very much alive and for all the world like one of those pre-historic animals you see in picture books . . . we first saw three humps in the water at about the centre of the river . . . The skin on it appeared deeply ridged, and at one point I saw what I took to be a neck like a big half-submerged tractor tyre'. It was visible for about six minutes; it travelled at a leisurely pace, rippling the water in passing, and showing about 15 ft of its body.

Whether the creature had slipped over Telford's weir, like a tadpole escaping from an over-filling jam-jar, or whether it had come up from the sea it is not possible to say. In defence of the two businessmen, one can turn back the pages of reports to 1936, when a Mr and Mrs Y. H. Hallam, of Filey, East Yorkshire, described seeing a 20 ft animal in the river Ness, showing a head and two humps and moving 'very fast' towards the sea. They were in a pleasure-boat at the time.

In late September 1965 I made another abortive attempt to gain close-up zoom photography, from the inaccessible place on the south shore east of Foyers Bay. It was my ninth private expedition; it nearly proved my last.

To avoid humping equipment through the trees and dense

undergrowth of the precipitous shoreline, a trek I had made on 124 occasions, I had brought a tiny fibreglass car-top boat. It proved most valuable, until I met a Loch Ness squall which almost capsized it. Next, ashore, I went down with some strange virus infection. My equipment kept going wrong, and I damaged my hand, almost losing the top joint of one finger.

Returning home, I felt so ill that I knew the time had come to abandon this wretched place, which had brought nothing but misfortune. In spite of the loch's seclusion I was conscious of something there, which did not seem rational: a subjective feeling of unease. It was as though some awful influence pervaded the atmosphere. Something evil.

Being an engineer, and therefore a practical person, I could not accept the dark forebodings of the ancient 'kelpie' legend, but instead decided to research the human history of the area, about which I knew little.

In due time, I did, and this proved both extraordinary and unexpected—exposing the bones of past events, which one could hardly even begin to suspect.

The following year I worked alone once more, but from the crescent beach of a tiny unmapped island—shared with a noisy flock of nesting oyster-catchers. Here, by contrast, I found only serenity of spirit—a place to which I could return at will, knowing it would be deserted by all but the wild creatures.

1965 was a year of poor weather; there were a few reports of sightings of 'tolerable authenticity', as recorded by the LNIB. Forty were accepted in 1963, eighteen in 1964, and only nine in 1965. But in other ways it was significant.

Dr Roy P. Mackal, an associate professor of biochemistry at the University of Chicago, visited the Ness to examine the evidence at first hand. He met David James, and was invited to join the LNIB as a director. Later he was to accomplish a great deal in the United States, attracting interest, and obtaining funds to help with the research.

A LNIB sequence of 35 mm. film showing two converging wakes was submitted for analysis to the RAF. The information obtained from this by their experts in photography was so encouraging that David James suggested they should examine my 1960 sequence which I had carefully preserved. This I was glad to agree to, knowing the Joint Air Reconnaissance Intelligence Centre (JARIC) had the very best equipment, and a reputation for accuracy. I sent them the original film, with a covering report.

In January 1966 their 'Photographic Interpretation Report No. 66/1' was submitted to the LNIB, in confidence; but the press had got to hear of it, and made comment, though not without some misinterpretation. It was necessary in consequence to publish the report in full, and this was done as a Crown copyright pamphlet, with an introduction by David James. The result was immediate, for within the covers of this 2,000-word technical analysis conclusions had been drawn which made the Monster scientifically *respectable*, for the first time in its long and chequered history!

The report accepted the film as genuine and on the basis of pure mensuration of the original filmed image stated that the object seen was neither a surface boat nor a submarine—'which leaves the conclusion it is probably an animate object'. When first on the surface it stood 3 ft high; allowing for some underwater bulk, 'a cross section through the object would be *not less* than 6 feet wide and 5 feet high'. At first there had been some confusion over estimates of length. No estimates were made in the report. Allowing for the niceties of photogrammetric work, and interpretation, and for certain criteria applying to the solid object filmed, which had both height and width, it was stated that the 'residual length in the horizontal plane would be in the order of 12 to 16 feet'. The speed of the object was estimated as between 7 and 10 m.p.h. as a mean. When first seen it was 1,667 yards distant, as opposed to the 1,300 yards I estimated from the map.

Perhaps the most astonishing thing about the report was its accuracy. Bearing in mind the subject material, a tiny granular dot on a 16 mm. rectangle of film, and the distance, an error of 1 inch in about 7,200 was established, and this conservatively! The boat I had sent out afterwards for deliberate comparison could be used as a yardstick. Its length was estimated at 13.3 ft in the report; in fact it measured 14 ft. Indeed the boat had proved most useful. Although it had been blandly ignored by one persistent critic, who said the object *was* a boat, JARIC thought otherwise. 'The object appears to submerge, but it can be readily argued that under certain conditions of light, reflectivity and aspect angle, etc., objects may not be visible on the photography. The boat was photographed on the same morning and light conditions were probably reasonably similar. When travelling parallel to the shore the boat is discernible as a boat shape and can be measured, whereas with the object there is *no* visible sign at all (paragraph 12).'

The JARIC report was invaluable. I was the more grateful too, for having had to wait six years for it. As so often happens, one success was followed by another. In June 1966 my second book, *The Leviathans*, was published, and I was invited to tour the four main Scottish universities, and speak to their biological societies. As an aero-engineer I felt somewhat out of place; but these lectures produced a stream of volunteers for the LNIB, and led to other invitations from universities in Britain, in Europe and ultimately the United States. *The Leviathans* was also reviewed on television. It contained a number of strange reports which had come to me concerning 'monsters' in the sea, and in lakes and rivers the world over; and more data on the Ness, including two new 'out of water' stories. It had been great fun writing the book: a labour of love. But the research was time-consuming and distracted my attention. I was not sorry to finish it.

In 1966 the LNIB mounted another full-length expedition, from May to October. Infra-red film was used, with which it was hoped to penetrate the mist which had in the past ruined sequences of film. But again, in spite of some good anti-cyclonic weather, and some twenty-nine accredited sightings, no new film was obtained.

I was no more fortunate working from 'the Island' as I had come to call it. This time I worked with a friend, a remarkable man who had mounted a lonely expedition at Loch Morar the year before. John Addey and I tried out various inducements, including *asafoetida*, a somewhat noxious compound, but without result—and at the very moment when a sighting was reported from a small ship almost opposite to us, we were distracted by a squall of rain, which blew our shelter down and put the cameras out of action. The LNIB missed it too, as described in their 1966 annual report. 'We had a singular disappointment on 21 August, when the pharmaceutical exhibition yacht, *Pharma*, on passage through the loch to Scandinavia, reported three sightings on the quarter, the last of which was immediately below H.Q. Unhappily our cameras are 190 ft above the surface of the loch and the cloudbase was 150 ft, so, although the vessel was duly logged through, the surface of the loch could not be seen'.

As if this near-miss wasn't sufficient, almost the same thing happened again in 1967, when I made two more visits to the Island. Once I marooned myself alone for a ten-day watch without ever going 'ashore'. Once, as a part of a holiday, I brought my family. They stayed at Foyers Hotel, but my eldest son and I camped on the Island for a couple of nights. Very early one brilliant sunny morning the back of the Monster was seen from a boat, which had been out drifting all night for the LNIB. It was near to us, but once again our attention was distracted by equipment. The episode was maddening, and later in September I retired back up the shore to watch from the place where I had started, seven years before. I needed time to think.

Events during the summer had not all been discouraging. I had won a splendid scientific award from Kodak, placing in my hands specialized ciné equipment. This freed me from the crippling costs of hiring cameras, and even more important, extended the time I could spend in the field. The LNIB expedition had also scored a bull's-eye with one of their long-range ciné rigs. They obtained a beautifully clear piece of 35 mm. black and white film showing a V wake developing, and moving over a glassy surface; *Scot II*, a converted steam-tug well known on the Ness, appeared conveniently in frame.

Thanks also to the untiring efforts of Professor Roy Mackal in the United States, the Field Enterprises Educational Corporation of Chicago made a large research grant to the Bureau. The Highlands and Islands Development Board in Scotland added £1,000 to this.

In 1968, therefore, the hunt was resumed with fervour. A number of long-range film sequences were obtained by the main expedition on black and white film, but none of them was adequately clear.

I spent the year on an excitingly different project, resulting from the thought I had given to the problem. It involved a catamaran—a big one, nearly 30 ft in length, and 14 ft in the beam. I had never sailed a canoe, but after nine months of frustration and enquiry I travelled up to the Clyde for a training cruise in an 8-metre Bobcat. It was a marvellous experience in brilliant weather, and after some thirty hours at sea in her I arranged a private charter. *Cizara* was owned by a Scots engineer and his family, all of whom were sailing enthusiasts. After a summer cruise among the Western Isles she was sailed up to Fort William, the western entrance to the Caledonian Ship Canal.

At Corpach basin I and my own family went aboard her. With Mr Ian Smith as skipper we took the 8-metre cat. some forty miles through the many locks, through Loch Lochy and Loch Oich to the Ness. It was a serenely beautiful passage. We tied up in the Ness before sailing the length of it, anchoring overnight at Foyers Bay and Glenurquhart. Then we returned to Fort Augustus where Ian Smith and my family departed, leaving me to 'loner' the Ness, with its dark and treacherous waters, for the next two weeks. Again, it was a marvellous experience, flavoured by the danger of sudden squalls, the rockbound coast—and the loneliness.

During this period, in September, my family and Mr Smith had gained a glimpse of a large humped object moving on the water at Inchnacardoch Bay, shortly after sunset. Twice we had encountered inexplicable wave disturbances as though some large object was moving through the water; but again, there was no photography.

Unquestionably, in 1968 the prize went to underwater research, and the people connected with it. In August the Department of Electronic and Electrical Engineering of the University of Birmingham, led by Professor D. Gordon Tucker and Hugh Braithwaite, a senior research associate, tried out a new type of digital sonar. A narrow acoustic emission was beamed across the loch from a jetty at Urquhart Bay. One frame of 16 mm. film was exposed every ten seconds, co-ordinated with a sound pulse and its response. Three objects, or groups of objects, were recorded. They were designated A, B and C, in the article prepared for the *New Scientist*, 19 December 1968. It was reprinted in the LNIB annual report of that year.

Object A was a 'large object' which rose some way from the bottom at a velocity of about 100 ft per minute; its 'velocity components along the axis of the sonar' reached about 6.5 knots maximum. It then almost disappeared out of the beam sector; then it descended to the bottom, and ascended again at about 120 ft per minute. Object B could possibly have been a shoal of fish swimming at constant depth. Object C . . .

is more startling. It appears only in frames 16 to 18 but has a horizontal velocity component along the range axis of the order of 7.5 m/s or 15 knots while diving at 2.4 m/s or 450 ft per minute. It appears to have a length of several metres.

Since the objects A and C are clearly comprised of animals, is it possible they could be fish? The high rate of ascent and descent makes it seem very unlikely, and fishery biologists we have consulted cannot suggest what fish they might be. It is a temptation to suppose they must be the fabulous Loch Ness monsters, now observed for the first time in their underwater activities! The present data, while leaving this as a possibility, are quite inadequate to decide the matter. A great deal of further investigation with more refined equipment—which is not at present available—is needed before definite conclusions are drawn.

We wish to acknowledge the help of our colleague Dr D. J. Creasey, and assistance with local arrangements and finance from the Loch Ness Phenomena Investigation Bureau.

Thus the report ended. It made no claims or statements it could not reasonably substantiate; it was treated lightly by the press, and on TV—almost with derision.

In 1969 the LNI (as it was now more conveniently referred to) started work again. There was a whirl of publicity accompanying the arrival of a small one-man submarine, shipped over from the United States. It was sponsored by *World Book Encyclopaedia* of Chicago. Built, owned and piloted by a likeable Texan, Dan Taylor, *Viperfish* was painted yellow, and attracted immediate attention. Dan was almost lost to sight beneath the barrage of pressmen and photographers. When after a long delay the submarine was launched in Urquhart Bay her failure to dive at once was not too well received. She was intended to home on echo responses from the motorized yacht *Rangitea,* which carried a mobile sonar probe, but in this event technical problems prevented this. However *Viperfish* did operate, and in this her experienced submariner pilot demonstrated courage.

Another larger and more sophisticated underwater vehicle called *Pisces* was also in the loch; it logged forty-seven dives, totalling some 250 hours on the bottom. She was being tested in a deep freshwater environment, and made a number of discoveries: registering a new depth maximum (on sonar) of 970 ft; maintaining U.H.F. (surface-radio) contacts down to 120 ft; photographing bottom trenches and craters, previously unsuspected; and being swirled around at 750 ft in an almost circular crater current! She also found a wreck, and animate creatures far below the usual fish levels. At 350 ft there was a small, white, plaice-like fish burrowing through the silt, and at 820 ft a 4-inch white eel. She saw some ancient weapons too, dumped into the silt of Urquhart Bay. But perhaps most interesting to the LNI was an occurrence at 500 ft. *Pisces* was hovering 50 ft above the bottom when she picked up a sonar target. She was piloted towards it, but the target rapidly disappeared from the screen at a range of

400 ft. Captain R. W. Eastaugh submitted a full account of her activities to the LNI, and this was published in the 1969 annual report. It was a most valuable contribution.

Other underwater work in 1969 included a week-long charter by the LNI of the drifter *Penorva*. A profile of the loch was made with an echo-sounder. She also trolled the bottom for giant eels, rumours of which had for so long existed. The sonar results were useful, but the fishing was abortive, though three hooks were lost from long lines. The crews included Major Eustace Maxwell, David James, and two zoologists from the University of Newcastle and the Royal Scottish Museum. This small group of experts showed how seriously the research was being taken.

From July until the third week in September I lived on the surface of the loch in a small cabin-cruiser called *Water Horse*. It had a 16 ft fibreglass hull with good freeboard, a big cockpit, and a tiny weatherproof cabin. The boat was a compromise: *Cizara* was not available for charter, and it had proved impossible to find another catamaran, because Loch Ness is so far north. The cabin-cruiser was procured for me by a helper at my home in Reading who was intrigued by the research—a splendid Scot, dynamic, cheerful, who knew far more about boats and motors than I. His name was Jim Ewing: a friend indeed.

In order to stabilize the tiny boat I was to live in, I had built two outrigger arms. They were anchored to the hull, and I attached dust-bin lids to them which rode underwater. The result was hydraulic damping in the rolling plane, which enabled me to mount a tripod in the cockpit with my 'Cyclops' rig attached. This was the complicated set-up I had engineered the year before with sound and still and ciné cameras all working in unison, at my fingertips.

During the twelve weeks on the water I helped the LNI as surface liaison-boat with Dan Taylor's little submarine. Thus I got to know and like its pilot. Most of the work he did was in Urquhart Bay. On one occasion the craft was swirled round through 180 degrees when resting on the bottom. What caused this disturbance was anybody's guess, but it had a sobering effect on Dan, who had years of submarine experience. He was a quiet man, surrounded by the press, who gave him little peace. He managed the boat and its instruments with confidence, demonstrating a type of personal courage which was in itself a justification. Deep in the icy pitch-black waters of the Ness, sealed by pressure into *Viperfish*, he was alone, and inaccessible, whereas *Pisces* had

a crew of three and a range of emergency systems. All the submariners in 1969 deserved praise, but I had no desire whatever
to follow their pursuits.

Sleeping alone on the surface at night could be unnerving
at times; weather was the danger. I would go to sleep anchored in
the lee of a rocky shore, perhaps to wake at 2 or 3 a.m. in a gale,
the wind and rain whipping the surface to a frenzy with *Water
Horse* bucking ferociously. To start the engine, up anchor and
plunge across the loch to find another lee, in total darkness, was
an experience. But the long weeks and months of drifting, the
incredible beauties of dawn, the excitement and activity ashore
made up for it.

The film-makers were out. Mirisch Films had rented Urquhart
Castle, and built a five-ton animated model-monster to take part
in 'The Private Life of Sherlock Holmes'. The resulting activity
was dramatic, but it was spoiled to some extent when the model
sank in a gale. It plunged to the bottom, where, to quote a local
radio commentator, it went to join its 'ain folk'.

Walt Disney Productions also shot film over a two week period.
They were aided by the LNI, and 'independents' such as myself
and another monster-hunter, Ivor Newby. He had first dived as
a frogman in Loch Ness in the summer of 1960, and had been
returning ever since, sometimes for the LNI but latterly independently. He worked from a handsome 18 ft motor boat. He gained
the nickname 'Ivor the Diver' because apart from his talents as a
frogman, he kept falling in fully clothed—four times altogether.
We worked in close company from Urquhart Bay for more than
five weeks.

Ken Peterson, the producer, employed Eddie McConnell,
a talented Scots cameraman, and his team to do the shooting for
a TV colour documentary. It was expected to appear before a
vast audience at some time in the future.

In September Robert Love joined the LNI team. He was an
actively brilliant American electronics engineer and an expert on
underwater research. He fitted *Rangitea* with a Honeywell
Scanner II sonar, and during the next six weeks logged some 150
miles on end-to-end sonar searches, depth soundings etc. Bob's
previous visit to the loch had produced much data from the
watery environment; channel wall and bottom topography,
bottom samples, light measurement and underwater visibility,
temperature measurements and surface observations. He had done
his homework well. The sonar probings produced a number of

interesting contacts. One, on 10 October, appeared to be animate; it was tracked for 2 minutes 19 seconds, during which time it moved along a looping path ahead of the boat, between 210 and 540 ft down, a minimum of 150 ft above the bottom. Like the Birmingham University team the year before, Bob Love made no claims about the Monster, but his work proved a valuable contribution to the sonar record.

Other sonars were operated from Temple Pier, in Urquhart Bay. The Birmingham team operated one for the LNI, and another was worked by the Plessey group of companies, in conjunction with Independent Television News and the *Daily Mail*. In two weeks of operation, no unexplained targets were observed. This had a depressing effect on the general public's attitude, because the work had been given blanket coverage on television. Plessey used a powerful *audible* sonar frequency, the loud 'pinging' from which echoed up and down the loch. Birmingham University's fixed-beam sonar scan depended for results on targets moving through it. The noise of boats and propellers as well the racket underwater may have served to frighten the 'targets' off, instead of upwards as had been hoped. That was certainly my opinion, and it was shared by others who had studied the Monster's history and apparent reaction to audible sound.

Another possible hoax occurred at this time when a very large bone was found at Loch Ness. It is described with fitting candour by David James in his truly excellent annual report for the LNI in 1969, covering the year's hectic proceedings, and events.

Two more short but interesting sequences of 35 mm. film had been exposed by the LNI. They were both of wakes, and shot at considerable range. My own experience included water disturbances on five separate occasions, which were simply inexplicable. The scale and pattern of these ruled out fish, and boats. Subterranean tremors may have caused them, but it was difficult to imagine one of these 600 ft below which would create the phenomenon I saw. This was a circular pattern of ripples 6 inches high, on jelly-calm water stretching for half a mile, as though coming from a point in the middle, close to the surface! I filmed and photographed such a disturbance, knowing inwardly that unless something solid appeared to explain it, I was wasting my time.

But nothing did; after eighty-two days and nights spent alone on the water, in such a confined space, it was disappointing. I had enjoyed the hunt, which had given me contact with the

LNI, the film-makers, submariners, and the wonderful local people ashore. During it I had become accepted by the wild duck and waterbirds of Urquhart Bay, itself a natural compliment; it vindicated the trouble I had taken to camouflage the boat, and make it a floating 'hide'. It was an experience I would hardly forget—or repeat, unless it was necessary, because I had lost weight, and on one or two occasions had come close to losing my life.

I was invited to run the LNI for 1970 as Surface Photography Director. This would mean working closely with Bob Love, who was Underwater Research Director. I accepted.

After so many years working on my own—for reasons of economy, and efficiency too—the change would be a big one. The LNI fielded a team of over a hundred each year, and there would be the problem of feeding, and accommodating, and training the teams. There would be transport, engineering, and photographic difficulties I felt sure. If we were to do our best we must experiment with new ideas and methods.

During the winter of 1969 I became much involved with correspondence, writing to monster-hunters of long experience, inviting them to help weld a team together. The response was gratifying.

In November I travelled to Norfolk, the home county of Wing-Commander K. H. Wallis, C.ENG., A.F.R.AE.S. He was famous for his tiny one-man autogyros, which he designed and built himself. His demonstration flight and the examples he showed me of his air photography convinced me that air patrols should be the innovation for 1970. In due course a contract was signed. He agreed to fly for us at the Ness, over two periods, totalling one month's aerial observation, during the course of the season— with a complete range of cameras at the ready.

There was some risk of fragmentation of effort in 1970 due to the influx of new groups and individuals who had enthusiasm, but little else, to contribute. As David James was seeking re-election to Parliament he could not be much at the scene.

In the event 'Nessie in '70'—the catch phrase for the season— proved to be a success both in the human sense, and technically. The investigation lasted twenty-one weeks, from the last week in May to the third week in October. A great deal happened in this period and it is only possible to skip over events.

Air patrols, with Ken Wallis flying the autogyro, produced some good photography. He proved that the technique of stalking

K

from the air was feasible, although no monster-targets presented themselves. Boat patrols, using *Water Horse*, were more fortunate; on one patrol I and two others spotted a thick telegraph-pole like object streaking through the water, at a range of half a mile. After careful consideration we concluded this must have protruded 10 ft out of the water, and been about 1 ft thick. Unfortunately, the sighting was too brief for photography, but it provided the second visual contact with the Beastie in eleven years of fieldwork, and cheered me up considerably. The head and neck we had seen was evidently part of a live animal, and capable of great speed. It had moved across the surface to disappear behind an outcrop of shoreline, and when we motored up in the boat there was no evidence of anything on the surface.

During the summer work at Achnahannet included the building of a small harbour down below the site, to give protection to our workboats. We trained cameramen, and women, numbering perhaps a hundred, and dealt with the press, and makers of TV documentaries. There were also uncounted other activities which kept me busy from daybreak to dusk, every day of the week. It was exhausting, but rewarding—and in stark contrast to the years of lonely effort which had preceded it.

Great numbers of visitors passed through the LNI's small exhibition caravan, stopping out of curiosity to examine the displays and read through the information provided. They were fascinated, and many went on their way impressed by what they had learned, and in most cases showing obvious goodwill. This 'public relations' activity was popular with the expeditioners, many of whom were university students giving up their holidays to work with the LNI. Sitting behind the caravan counter, like a village shopkeeper, dispensing booklets and annual reports and answering questions endlessly made a break from the monotony of camera duty. Each expeditioner could expect one day out of two continuously on watch at the out-stations. Every other day they did 'second line' duty at base camp, which included public relations, camp chores, harbour building and the usual evening's entertainments. Quite rightly Achnahannet was 'dry'. It had to be, but traditionally there was no lack of good cheer at local hostelries; and as the teams of volunteers often included talented musicians, we enjoyed their accompaniment.

In 1969 Loch Morar, a little south of Loch Ness and close to the west Highland seaboard, had produced new evidence that it had a 'Nessie' of its own. In 1970 this was investigated at first hand by a team of young scientists and mature enthusiasts. The first Loch Morar Survey spent six weeks conducting an ecological study, to establish whether or not the loch could harbour a large unidentified species. The beast was nicknamed 'Morag'.

Loch Morar had a background of reports of sightings and a legend of a water kelpie. The most recent appearance I knew about was in 1964. Then in 1969 Morag was reported to have actually collided with a fishing boat. The Loch Morar Survey (LMS) had many volunteers who had worked with the LNI in previous years, and one in particular, Mrs Elizabeth Montgomery · Campbell*M.J.I., undertook to study the historical record, and do some on-the-spot research.

This proved dramatically successful, and Liz, who had worked as one of the most popular and effective group commanders at the LNI later published twenty-seven accounts of sightings in the first LMS report, released at a press conference at the Zoological Society in London. This included the findings of the highly scientific biological survey, incorporating floristic, faunistic and chemical survey work as a part of the basic study, to establish whether or not Morar could possibly sustain large aquatic animals.

The results of this study, although technically difficult for a layman to understand, indicated that the loch was rich in chemical nutrient, plankton and fish life. It was not a sterile body of water, and due to its size and great depth, physically there was room for such a species.

In view of this activity, and a personal interest in the goings-on at Morar, which I had never actually visited, I travelled there, taking *Water Horse* on a trailer. Ken Wallis came with me, and brought the autogyro. For a week he flew over the loch, and I scooted about its surface, experiencing for the first time the ecstatic joys of hydroplaning. My new 40-horsepower outboard engine lifted the small craft as it skimmed across the glassy surface of this mystical beautiful lake. Loch Ness was rugged, and on occasion it could produce effects of mist and mountain which were breathtaking—but Loch Morar had something of a dreamlike quality. It was also deserted, and had crystal clear water. There were no roads around it and access was limited to the western extremity. There were islands, coves and inlets, crystalline shingle beaches, great depths and shallows, and barbarous rocks,

* Co-author of the book *The Search for Morag* published by Tom Stacey, Ltd.
Dr David Solomon, a member of the committee of the *LMS*, contributed technically.

some of which were not charted. Ken Wallis spotted them from the air and marked them down on a map for me. They lay just beneath the surface.

Neither of us saw the monster, or even a disturbance. The only unusual event occurred at several thousand feet when the autogyro almost collided with a golden eagle!

Back at the Ness underwater research was proceeding under the direction of Bob Love, who had again returned with the sponsorship of Field Enterprises of Chicago, working through the LNI. He had many experiments to develop, and suffered the usual frustration caused by rough weather, snarled lines and equipment being blown away. He battled on, helped by a colourful and expert crew of technicians, radar specialists and divers—the latter were exploring the sunken wreck he had found in Urquhart Bay the year previously. It was thought that it might be a *Zulu*, a type of bluff-hulled sailing vessel designed at the time of the Zulu wars. It lay in the silt some 80 ft underwater, but sections from it showed the wood to be almost perfect, still giving off the faintly aromatic odour of resin. A thin outer skin of peat-stained fibres seemed to have preserved the wood beneath. This suggested that the water in Loch Ness with its heavy peat content might act as a preservative on other bodies too.

Bob Love scored a success at the very end of the season when his underwater listening equipment picked up strange rhythmic pulsations, which no one was able to identify. These curious sounds were thought to emanate from about 30 ft, but were picked up in many different places in Urquhart Bay. They seemed of the type and character produced as signals by underwater creatures— an animal sonar perhaps, but no one would commit himself. The experts were baffled.

Three other groups visited Loch Ness in 1970, as newcomers. Italian Television made a fine documentary for their *Aventura* series, working with the LNI from Achnahannet. The American importers of 'Black and White' Scotch whisky sponsored a small group armed with an infra-red camera device, who also worked through the LNI, and in particular Bob Love's underwater team at Urquhart Bay. They brought good humour and colour to the undertaking, but were thwarted to some extent by technical difficulties, and the short range of their device—which was barely a hundred yards. They departed expressing the desire to return with more powerful equipment.

In September Dr Robert H. Rines, President of the Academy

of Applied Science from Belmont, Massachusetts, arrived with a small team of electronic and sonar experts, equipped with underwater listening and playback apparatus. More importantly they brought a Klein Associates high-definition side-scan sonar. This marvellous device could be operated from a fixed position, or trailed from a moving craft; either way it was capable of recording 'intruders' clearly on a chart. Dr Martin Klein, the designer, was in attendance. A short time after the equipment had been attached to a small scaffolding pier extending into Urquhart Bay, two large intruders went through the sound-screen in one direction; a little later one returned from the opposite direction. These echoes did not appear to be from fish. They were of considerable size, and had a 'shape' which reversed when coming back through the screen. They did not appear to be spurious echoes and they were neither from divers, nor anchor chains.

The day following, because of the noise of boats and other interferences in Urquhart Bay, it was decided to trail the sonar further down the loch, where all was quiet and tranquil. I offered the use of *Water Horse*, because I had long suspected that there might be a 'resident' Monster in the vicinity of the south-western wall of the loch a mile or two from Fort Augustus. The sighting record suggested this, and I knew from experience that aquatic predators have a habit of patrolling sections of shoreline which become their territory. Male animals, particularly, tend to do this. Torquil MacLeod's sighting on land in this area suggested a very big animal, which would probably be a male.

For two days we trailed the side-scan sonar, or 'fish'. It was a curious-looking finned device which both transmitted sound impulses and received the echoes. It transformed these through electronic systems to appear as sepia stains on a wide sheet of chart paper. I watched the whole proceeding from the cockpit of little *Water Horse*, and was fascinated to see salmon and trout coming up as tiny pencil dots. The bottom, sidewall and surface echoes were recorded as definite lines and sepia shadings, on the double-sided chart. Each half of the chart painted out the echoes received from the fan-beam of pulsated sound emitted by the 'fish'. These were of too high a frequency for the human ear, but the pulses in air produced a sharp snapping sound, like someone snapping his fingers. Underwater these emissions sped outwards, and the reflections bounced back to be picked up by the device.

During the course of these patrols on several occasions the chart produced enormous blips—distinct echoes which did not appear to be false, and which were definitely in the 'watercolumn'.

One was in the great 700 ft trench which the sonar discovered immediately off shore, where Torquil MacLeod had seen the Monster in March 1960. I was not qualified to draw conclusions, but in both the preliminary and final reports of the Academy of Applied Science to the LNI it was stated that there 'are large moving objects in the Loch', and that 'there is abundant fishlife in the loch which could support a large creature'. The sonar also discovered clear evidence of ridges or cutbacks in the steep walls of the loch in this region. This latter conclusion was verified by a diver who visited the LNI information centre at Achnahannet in 1971, Mr J. K. Anderson of Stirling. He was kind enough to record details of the dive he and two companions made in June 1969 opposite Glenmoriston. In his letter he said,

'We crossed the loch in a rubber dinghy from Invermoriston . . . on entering the water we found visibility about 20–25 feet but this decreased as we descended owing to peat sediment causing light refraction. At a depth of 25 feet we encountered a large boulder. We climbed round and over this—still going down. Almost immediately underneath it we saw a cut-back or overhang approximately 5–6 feet wide. Owing to bad visibility we had no idea how far this extended in either direction. We bypassed this and at a depth of about 35–40 ft. saw another similar geological formation . . . At this time in our dive we saw there was no further point in going deeper owing to the decreasing visibility . . . I trust this information will be of some value to you.'

Neither the sonar operators nor the divers had any idea of each other's comments or conclusions. This helps to prove that the tendency to regard sonar results as spurious, and divers' reports as fanciful is unjustified. Experts do sometimes make mistakes, and divers do sometimes exaggerate, no doubt, but most of the time they are both accurate and truthful. In this case too they proved the age-old legend at Loch Ness that there are caverns underwater—although this might reasonably be expected, as the whole of the Great Glen is a colossal fault zone.

Two other events occurred in 1970 which helped to establish facts. The first concerned the natural fish population of the loch, and therefore had a bearing on food-chain; the second concerned a possible physical contact with the Monster underwater!

There was slight but positive evidence in Loch Ness for Arctic char, a type of deep swimming game-fish akin to the trout. It had been known for many years, but as these fish shoaled in the very deep water, 80–300 ft down, they were practically never seen. Indeed many local fishermen would have denied their existence with a knowing shake of the head. They had never caught one! In 1960 the first scientific work with echo-sounders was carried out by a group of students from Oxford and Cambridge; they picked up dense shoals of fish between 14 and 16 fathoms (80–95 ft). These were thought to be char. On the side-scan sonar in 1970 dense shoals were charted at depth, to which I was a witness. Bob Love also caught two such fish accidentally in eel traps in Urquhart Bay. An immensely experienced herring-boat skipper, who was piloting *Rangitea*, the LNI sonar boat, interpreted a giant shoal which came up on the fish-finder, as representing 'six ton of fish'. With his up-to-date experience using fish-finders commercially, he could be relied on to estimate correctly. As salmon and trout do not shoal like this in Loch Ness, the probability is they were Arctic char, in huge numbers.

Apart from the game fish, the loch contained an immense population of eels; when these were caught in traps some curious features were noticed. Eels of great age were caught, and some with light-coloured pigmentation, and one or two with peculiar fin arrangements. They provided the scientists, particularly Professor Roy Mackal at the University of Chicago, with some interesting data. The possibility that eels were an item on the Monster's menu had occupied the minds of scientists for years. One in particular, Dr Denys Tucker, propounded theories as to their character in Loch Ness as long ago as 1960. It was a logical step therefore to play back eel noises underwater in the hope these would attract the Beast. In 1970 the LNI tried this technique, and so did the Academy people, working from *Water Horse*, to supplement other baiting experiments using sex hormones, and various complex substances.

Some of these 'lures' were effective in an entirely different, and unexpected way. They attracted the attentions of the press, the word 'sex' acting like a homing beacon; cartoons and comments were published which were funny but not very enlightening. Among the American scientists who had helped to compound these harmless baits were some of the world's leading authorities on underwater life, and on the sophisticated analysis of hormones and other materials which were known to attract animals underwater. But the results of these experiments were difficult to assess.

They did not cause the Monster to surface, which was disappointing.

We tried a more simple technique of dumping pebbles, soaked in salmon oil, into the loch in the vicinity of the sonar-blips. This produced impressive areas of calm and, no doubt, streams of scent underwater which we hoped would bring the Monster up—but again without any obvious result. However, when lowering hydrophones in this area, in more than 600 ft of water, Mr Isaac S. Blonder of the Academy team had a very strange experience, which startled all of us.

The hydrophone went over the side, attached to the end of a 600 ft cable—but at about 200 ft its downward movement was checked by something solid. Ike Blonder was paying out the cable by hand, so there was no mistake about it. For a moment or two the hydrophone appeared to bounce and scrape over the obstruction, producing loud rasping noises aboard, through the speaker. I saw Bob Rines look up, his expression registering the thought we all had in our minds—could it be the Monster coming up to investigate? We were in exactly the right locality.

Mysteriously, the weighted line then continued to descend to over 600 ft without another pause. As this was a real experience there had to be a logical explanation. A waterlogged tree-trunk floating at 200 ft down seemed improbable. Kelts (spent salmon) are known to swim at great depth after the spawning process, but no such fish could have caused an obstruction like the one we had experienced. We felt a little anxious. A small 16-ft boat floating over a great trench of water and almost overhung by the towering cliffs of Loch Ness, is not the most reassuring platform.

The light was fading, and we had some miles to go to get back to Fort Augustus. We arrived in the dark, tied up, and clambered ashore reeking of salmon oil and the more exotic scents exuding from the sex hormones, which hung thickly in the boat.

In due time tape-recordings made in the vicinity of the trench were analysed by the Academy team and their associates. It was found that pulse-like emissions had been recorded showing double 5 milli-second bursts in the 4–8 kilohertz range. The possibility that these were an animal sonar could be neither ruled out nor established positively, but in view of our experience with the hydrophone we kept an open mind about it. There are predators underwater which have developed such a system to help them hunt their prey.

The end of the 1970 activities based on Achnahannet, came in late October with the first of the roaring equinoctial gales. Late on the evening of the 22 October wind force rose until gusts of 100 miles per hour battered the camp, smashing trailers and equipment. Fortunately only the few remaining resident staff were on site and no one was injured—but as a result of this experience I decided that should I be invited to run the expedition in 1971, I would end the hunt in mid-September.

In the winter months there was always much to do, and as I had been working full-time on the research since the catamaran expedition in 1968 the pattern was familiar. However in April 1971 the Academy of Applied Science made arrangements for me to address audiences in the eastern United States, as an introduction to the subject.

I flew to Boston, and spent a hectic few weeks travelling about under the direction of its president, the dynamic Robert Rines. It proved a vortex of activity, and from it flowed both technical support and interest. Isaac Blonder, at the Blonder Tongue Laboratories, showed me the sophisticated tape and hydrophone sets he had developed, with 'playback' built into them, designed to repeat underwater sonar noises back to the source, upon receiving them. This it was hoped would tend to excite the curiosity of the Monster, assuming it proved to be the source. At the Massachusetts Institute of Technology Professor Harold Edgerton, famed for his pioneering work in underwater strobe-light photography, undertook to modify one of his cameras to suit the Ness environment.

Interviews on TV and radio, and with the press, including the *New York Times*, helped me to make a case for continuing observation and I was grateful to my many different hosts for their hospitality. America I found to be a place of human dynamism, with a most refreshing attitude towards the learning process and, of course, technology.

Back in Britain I had barely one week in which to re-orient myself and prepare for the coming offensive. I was exhausted and the LNI in 1971 would give me little chance to recuperate. In the absence of Robert Love, I would have to run both the shore-watch and the underwater work—in fact, the whole operation. It was a daunting prospect; but once I got back to Loch Ness, the fresh air and exercise, the glorious early summer weather, and the ever-present currents of excitement served to revive my spirits.

It proved to be another year in which a whole range of activities took place. New ideas and experiments, superseded each other. Every day brought its variations, introductions and moments of excitement. People who were now coming into the LNI at Achnahannet with their sighting accounts, sometimes within minutes of the experience would tape them for us; often the drama was evident. I had long known that real witnesses, if close to the event in time, would unconsciously demonstrate the fact. Their hands shook a little, and this could not be faked, because only fear, or shock or extreme nervous excitement produces this effect in healthy people.

June and July produced a number of sightings. Some saw the head, neck and humps at close range. Others described humps or backs at a distance, or simply wakes. Not all were acceptable, but with the small cassette tape-recorders we possessed, this information, backed up by the standard sighting-report forms, soon began to accumulate.

Photographically we appeared to be getting closer to the Monster—some of the near misses were so close in time or locality we felt certain that our luck must change. But, inexorably, the odds continued to defeat us, as they had in previous years. Our ever-watchful long-range camera crews could do no more than train, and maintain a state of preparedness. It was maddening, On two occasions cameras had been in one place one day and another the next, only to find the move had robbed us of photography. It was difficult not to fall into a state of despondency— or begin to believe some of the older people who would shake their heads and mutter seriously 'ye'll neverrr film the Beast.'

Disregarding the fact we had already done so, on several occasions—though admittedly at too great a range—this dire warning secretly had an effect on people. The Loch Ness 'hoodoo' was something which bordered on the realms of both fact and fantasy, and it was difficult not to tally up the small misfortunes which had robbed us of photography. The 'hoodoo' seemed to affect people connected with the research; several had experienced an incredible near-miss at one time or another, or knew someone else who had. I had endured several near-misses over the years and in 1971 it happened twice more; but with the arrival of Bob Rines from the Academy, in America thoughts of failure were dismissed. He carried with him the enthusiasm and the technical assurance which are part of the American way of life; more important still, he brought Professor Harold Edgerton's marvellous underwater flashing ciné camera.

We put it to work, testing both in Loch Ness, and in the swimming pool at Inverness, to simulate the crystal waters of Loch Morar. Operations started first in Urquhart Bay, using *Fussy Hen* the LNI's work boat. Then we attached the equipment to buoys and left it unattended, taking pictures underwater through the hours of darkness.

Every precaution was taken to anchor the equipment safely on the bottom and mark it with buoys to support it if it drifted into deep water. But at first light next morning there was no sign of it. It had disappeared completely.

Much dismayed by this I ordered the assistance of two professional divers from Inverness. They spent an hour or two plunging into the inky depths only to find the shallows in which the camera had stood bordered on a precipitous underwater cliff.

We concluded that the strobe-light camera had either been towed out by salmon poachers (who work at night) and cut adrift from the marker buoys, to sink—or that, just conceivably, it had been towed away by the Beast, which had become entangled in the cordage.

Grappling with hooks from a boat in the hopes of snagging the ropes underwater was unsuccessful. But when the boat was on its way back to Achnahannet the steersman found two of the buoys a mile or so away, drifting down the middle of the loch. He pulled up the camera, and found it undamaged. How it had got there was a mystery. When the film was developed it proved that the camera had remained underwater for the whole time. The only thing that appeared on the pictures was loops of the rope which had attached the camera to the buoys. There were no poachers' faces, and no pictures of the Monster either.

Later Bob Rines and I worked with the equipment on Loch Morar, where I spent a week living on *Water Horse*. It was a busman's holiday for me, but one I enjoyed immensely. The loch in all its fantastic beauty offered as much of a challenge as Loch Ness. The Loch Morar Survey team was hard at work with its ecological and biological studies continuing from the year before. Several were from the LNI, and as I was by now a member of the LMS Committee it was encouraging to have them.

Mr Isaac Blonder—the inimitable 'Ike'—and his elder son Greg came with us to Morar, on behalf of the Academy, bringing with them a mass of hydrophone and tape equipment. I had them aboard *Water Horse* and for days we worked hard listening through stereophonic ears underwater, and mapping the bottom to aid the

LMS crews who were sampling it. We spent nearly three whole days drifting and moving about the surface, most of the time wallowing badly as I had not brought stabilizers. Ike was a poor sailor, but stoically insisted on staying aboard. There was some technical trouble, and on one occasion we nearly hit a rock at 20 knots. Morar had many rocks, which posed a threat to fast-moving boats. The marker pole on this one had been bent over by some fool of a practical joker, or possibly by another boat. We missed it by no more than a few feet. It would have ripped the bottom out of *Water Horse*.

Work with the strobe-light camera posed a problem, for there was no room to spare in *Water Horse*. She was at best a one-man boat but, by dint of much squeezing away of equipment and tidying up, I contrived to make her a home for Bob Rines and myself overnight. through some truly fearsome weather. We moved up loch, with the dark waves sweeping past, loaded to the gunwales. The boat rolled and pitched about but we contrived to lower the camera to the bottom, leaving it there to blink away all night. In the morning the conditions had much improved. Bob loaded the camera with colour film, and when this was developed we found the photography to be excellent, with rocks and boulders visible at a range of 60 ft. Again, there was no 'intruder'—but we had mastered the technique which, with the crystal water in Morar promised well for the future.

Back at Loch Ness the season progressed, with huge numbers of people visiting the information centre at Achnahannet, which we had developed considerably. In all more than 50,000 people went through in 1971.

In early August one of the LNI expeditioners had a strange and disturbing experience in Urquhart Bay, while swimming under-water in a frogman suit. 'Brock' Badger claimed four years' experience in monster-hunting. He was a big, cheerful young Scot of the type who make an expedition. Reliable and hard-working, he was liked by everyone. Because he had underwater experience, he volunteered to help put down a mooring for the LNI's new workboat *Narwhal*. A small work-party brought the blocks of concrete in by truck, and floated these out to dump them in position by cutting the securing ropes. The mooring was rigged, and the crew returned ashore. Brock stayed behind to enjoy a few minutes' swimming and diving underwater. My eldest son, Simon, on leave from the army was among the work party. On turning round he noticed the surface erupt, and Brock surfaced and swam back to shore at a great speed. He had seen something large and 'cylindrical' moving in front of him. He reckoned it was 6 ft in diameter, without visible protuberances; it extended beyond his vision through the face-mask on either side. It appeared to be moving slowly from right to left. He did not wait to investigate.

This experience had a noticeable effect on the Scot. He became subdued, so quiet that we thought he was feeling unwell. It was not until two days afterwards that I questioned him about it. He had made no attempt to publicize his experience, even among the expedition people. At the time he had merely said 'I thought I saw something underwater', adding that he 'wouldn't go back in the water'. As he was in no more than 15–20 feet of water at the time, some felt it was too shallow for the Monster, but I did not consider this to be the case. I was absolutely convinced of Brock's sincerity, and his ability to describe his experience objectively. I knew the Monster had been seen close to shore in Urquhart Bay on many occasions. At the season's end Bob Rines, working with an echo-sounder, found that the bay shelved precipitously right round its perimeter. Then I realized that this curious underwater bowl shape would allow the Beast to patrol the shallow edge, and yet remain in deep water. The degree of shelving was acute; in some places only yards from the shore the water was 70 ft deep.

Later in 1971 I became involved in more bizarre experiments, helping to employ various devices from the surface of the loch in *Water Horse*. Baits of all kinds were tried: foods, sex lures, sonar targets and searching devices, and stimulating electromagnetic waves. We used listening and sound-transmitting devices—and tried music too. The latter experiment I engineered through a tape-recorder and underwater speaker. I spent many langorous hours cradled on the surface listening to the glorious refrains of Beethoven's Sixth Symphony ringing underwater but, alas, to no visible effect. Like all the other experimenters (some of whom were much assured of success) we only proved what a very difficult target we had chosen.

However, on 6 September, quite unexpectedly the Beast exposed itself, though only momentarily. I was motoring *Water Horse* through rough water towards Foyers Point, to try out a new baiting technique. It was mid-afternoon, and stormy, and the surface noise from the hydro-works at Foyers was loud enough. Out of the corner of my eye I spotted a black snake-like object rear above the water; it stayed erect for a moment, then it was

Figure 19   My sighting, 6 September 1971.

quickly withdrawn. By now I was staring full-face, spellbound, towards the object—unbelievingly. Surely it *couldn't* be the Monster. After so many fruitless years of searching, my mind simply rejected the possibility.

I continued to stare, only to see it again break surface, then go down in a boil of white foam. It was no more than 200 yards distant—I could judge by the size of seagulls.

Too late I throttled back, then crept forward over the loch towards Foyers Point. There were five cameras in front of me. Because of my rooted attention to the place where the neck had broken surface I ran the boat aground. Fumbling angrily with throttles, I poled off and dropped anchor, throwing the bait bag overside. It was clear that unless I could get hold of myself I would never film a thing. I put on my life-jacket.

In due time a report was published in the national press, and on radio: I had switched on a small tape-recorder only moments after the sighting, to make a commentary. The result was real enough, but there had not been time to take photographs. Mentally I had suffered a shock, and because of it I began to train myself to use a camera without any sighting process, aiming it like a sub machine gun. I was convinced, now, that a close-range sighting was so dramatic, so mesmeric in effect, that it would inhibit any camera drill which tended to obscure one's vision. The process of aiming and shooting through a restrictive camera sight would be almost impossible at close quarters.

The next day I checked on seagulls swimming at a distance, and confirmed my ranging estimate as approximately correct. It was 200 yards, or just a little over; and a pair of swans moving towards me in Urquhart Bay conveniently gave a clue to size. They seemed minute in comparison.

The live object I had seen was between 4 and 6 ft out of the water. It was mobile, muscular—and for a moment of time almost exactly similar to the 'Surgeon's Photograph'. The one difference was in the extremity, which had no visible features; it appeared rounded like the end of a worm. It was suggested afterwards to me the object might have been a tail, but I rejected this. If it was a tail, then it was moving backwards!

In mid-September the last LNI team departed. Whereas before they had always been replaced by other eager faces, there was no one. Just a blank—a dreadful emptiness. I myself returned south for a week, to recuperate and recover my enthusiasm, before travelling back to attend to business and the winding-up procedure. Running an expedition of the size, and duration, fielded by the LNI was no small undertaking, and there was a mass of details to be sorted out.

I was determined to gain a few days monster-hunting entirely by myself, down at the south-western end of the loch, away from everybody. I trailed my caravan out and for a day or two parked it near Alex Campbell's cottage. Alex was now retired after having been a water bailiff for forty-five years; our friendship starting on that fateful day in 1960 had never diminished.

I moored *Water Horse* in the mouth of the river Oich, but I had to move her when a storm developed and brought torrents of brown water roaring down in spate. For a day or two she stood at the Abbey jetty, while I watched from a private strip of land owned by the canal authority.

Bob Rines appeared once more. We had hoped to go back to Morar, but time was short, and the weather impossible. I had intended to pull the boat out but spent the morning buffeting about on the loch, drenched with rain and rattled at by hailstones. It simply was not practicable. Morar had to wait for another year. Bob departed to his base in Drumnadrochit from which he continued strobe-light photography and the mapping of Urquhart Bay, working from the deck of *Narwhal*. She was an old lifeboat from the *Britannic*, a Cunarder scrapped after the World War II. In May I had decided to renovate her, and the LNI had done the work during the summer. She looked splendid in a coat of spotless paint, mounting a side transom and a five-bladed outboard motor. She weighed several tons. There was an extension keel for sailing, and now a deck house, giving protection. *Narwhal* was a most unusual-looking craft, with a bowsprit and other peculiar features —but she was safe on Loch Ness, and ideal for working experiments.

I was alone once more, with three days in which to concentrate on watching. The weather changed, producing marvellous sunshine, flat calm, and at night paralysing cold. I awoke in my caravan, shivering at 3 a.m. There was ice in my saucepan. In the morning the shore was white with frost, and tendrils of mist swirled over the great pool of water. The effect was one of unreality—dreaming almost. I knew if the Monster surfaced no one would believe photography with such a fantastic setting. They would think it was a fake—a model in a tank. I was glad when the sun burned away the mist and exposed the loch in all its rugged splendour.

The day of 13 October passed slowly. I knew the conditions were right for the Monster to surface—'Nessie weather' we called it—and I sensed that I could be close to it. My position was good, but the light was wrong until about midday, when the wintry sun passed behind me at a very flat angle. Loch Ness was a long way north. I had intended to use *Water Horse* to get 'up sun' in the morning but did not accomplish this. Watching alone involves a host of minor chores, cooking, and other distractions, and boat work is time-consuming.

That evening Miss Turner, who was secretary to the nearby Abbey, was introduced to me. At midday she had stopped on her way towards Inverness when she had noticed a crowd of people looking towards the loch. I taped her account.

> Just before I came into Invermoriston I saw a lot of people looking at the loch, and I saw a distinct line, or cut, right through the water, which was like glass—running for about a quarter of a mile; and then whatever it was turned round and there was really a *terrific* turbulence. I saw no head, or no object, but *something* caused that—and there were no boats anywhere . . .

I questioned Miss Turner further, and asked whether the wake was coming in my direction. She said that it was, to start with, but it appeared to have turned round. The disturbance was more than half way across the loch; which would have made it about half a mile distant.

I was encouraged by this obviously factual account. The next morning, which again was sunlit and misty, I set up my battery of cameras on the tripod to await developments. I was convinced that my position would be good for photographs, but as the boat was sheathed in frost, like sparkling icing-sugar, I again failed to make use of it to get the sun behind me. In consequence, for much of the morning the water to the south was lost in a blaze of reflected sunlight, which blinded me when I attempted to peer through it.

At some time after 11 a.m. I noticed a tall monk stride down towards the Abbey jetty, across the Caledonian Canal. There was someone with him, and he had a camera slung over his shoulder. He pointed and I could just hear his voice, saying that he had 'seen movement'. I called across, hoping to find out more of what he knew, but due to some trick of acoustics he could not hear me, and as I was blinded by the light in that direction it made little difference. I redoubled my efforts to concentrate, but that afternoon the anticyclonic patch of weather moved away, and was replaced by a steadily mounting wind. Inwardly, I knew that my last chance in 1971 had gone with it. I drifted in the boat until the light began to fade; once more I noted the coloured leaves of autumn, suspended in the water, turning over slowly in my wake. For some reason these jewels of natural colour affected me— pathos swept over me. It was the end, the death of another season, with all its life force spent: inexpressibly sad.

Back on shore, I began to slowly put my things together. There was so much equipment, and I was weary of it all.

The day following, in very rough water I moved the boat round to Inchnacardoch Bay, and pulled her out. *Water Horse* was sheathed in a fine peat-coloured growth of algae. The hull was scratched and chipped in places, the marks of a summer's work. I had grown absurdly fond of her, but I knew that equipment must always serve a purpose, and that it must ruthlessly be replaced if better gear becomes available.

I trundled her back to Drumnadrochit for winter storage, stopping *en route* at Achnahannet. There I learned that on the morning previously, about half an hour before I had seen the tall monk, Father Gregory, and another witness had watched the Monster's head and neck rear 10 ft out of the water at the centre of a great disturbance. They had been only a few hundred yards from it. I had not seen this because the blazing sunlight, glittering off the water, had blinded me. Because I had failed to use the boat to get 'up sun' of the Monster I had lost a sequence of film

L

which would have proved the marvellous truth of the creature's existence for everyone to witness.

After eleven years of work, through nineteen expeditions with this simple objective as the spur to action, my failure to achieve it was very hard to bear. The misfortune of it stunned me—it was a blow beneath the belt, which knocked me to the canvas. And yet, I had no one to blame but myself. Common sense had warned me to get the sun behind me and I had failed to take the necessary action. In all honesty I could not blame the Loch Ness 'hoodoo' for that.

Later I was to learn that shortly after Miss Turner's experience on 13 October several people had reported seeing humps and a very big V wake from a place eastwards of her sighting point. Among them were two policemen, a sergeant and an inspector.

Holly Arnold, the young American who was secretary to the LNI had obtained reports from them, and excellent tape-recordings. She also obtained one from Father Gregory. I listened to them, and realized that in this trilogy of witnesses' reports there might be found the key to modern credibility. No one could honestly doubt such people, or their ability to describe what they had seen. For this reason it would be doubly important to publish these accounts, exactly as recorded.

Police Inspector Henry Henderson, of 208 Old Edinburgh Road, Inverness, Scotland, recorded in his LNI sighting-report form that the estimated overall length of the object was 25–30 ft; it was travelling at 10–15 m.p.h. from west to east in a straight line. It was about half way across the loch, at a point half a mile east of the Altsigh Youth Hostel. It was visible to him and his co-witness, Sergeant George W. Mackenzie, from '1415 hrs. to 1417 hrs.'

The first thing noticed was a wave pattern coming towards the shore below us. The water was flat calm and a 'V' shaped wave pattern was coming in from about the centre of the loch. The first wave would have been about two feet high. Following the wave outwards I saw two large black coloured 'humps' about 10–12 feet behind the point where the 'V' parted. I would say that there would be at least six to eight feet between the 'humps' . . . the impression was quite definite that they were connected below the surface. The objects were visible for two minutes at which time they appeared to go lower and lower in the water and gradually

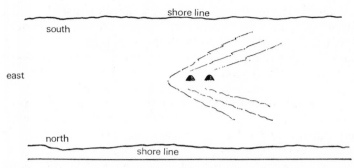

Figure 20   Sketch drawn by Inspector Henderson of his sighting, 13 October 1971.

disappeared. The significant point in this was that the water then returned to flat calm condition . . . the objects gave the impression of two large seals or dolphins sporting, but this was only an initial impression—as time went on it became obvious that the two objects were part of one large animate object. Seen travelling over a distance of about half a mile.

Sergeant George Mackenzie, of 152 Bruce Gardens, Inverness, filled out a sighting report independently. He said much the same about the experience, although his estimate of size was bigger. He thought the overall length was '30–40' ft. He said that waves about '4 feet in height', caused by the two-humped object, broke on the shore after its submergence. He estimated that both humps were 'five feet' out of the water. Both men said that there were no craft in the vicinity.

Shortly after I returned home to Berkshire I wrote to Father Gregory asking for his account, and if possible a sketch. He replied:

October 19th 1971

Dear Mr. Dinsdale,

Many thanks for your letter. It was rather unfortunate that you missed sharing this sighting with us, but I was glad to hear of your own evidence, particularly about the height of the neck—and to be able to corroborate this for you! I hope the enclosed account of our experience is what you want . . .

Yours sincerely,
Gregory Brusey.
The Abbey, Fort Augustus, Inverness-shire.

On Thursday morning, October 14th, I took a friend,
Mr. Roger Pugh, the organist and choirmaster of St. James,
Spanish Place, London, down to the loch-side to admire
the view. It was a bright sunny day, and the loch surface
was calm and untroubled by any boats. Standing on the
stone jetty near the boat house we looked towards Borlum
Bay, when suddenly there was a terrific commotion in the
waters of the bay. In the midst of this disturbance we saw
quite distinctly the neck of the beast standing out of the
water to what we calculated later to be a height of about
10 feet. It swam towards us at a slight angle, and after about
twenty seconds slowly disappeared, the neck immersing at a
slight angle. We were at a distance of about 300 yards,
which prevented us from seeing any of the humps of the
beast had they been exposed.

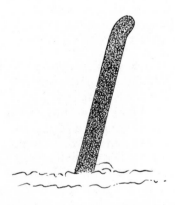

Figure 21   Sketch drawn by Father Gregory Brusey of his sighting,
14 October 1971.

I read this letter, and the report which accompanied it, signed
by both witnesses, and examined the sketch. Somehow all the
disappointment ebbed away from me. It helped me to pick myself
up from the canvas once more, for in the light of such a marvellous
natural mystery, time was unimportant, and therefore failure too.

I knew that in 1972 I would be able to go back to the loch, to
battle with the odds again, in the best of company. The voluntary
teams of the LNI, and the LMS, the Academy people—and the
many other individuals who in one way or another helped towards

our common objective, and a defence of what really mattered most—the simple truth.

Once this was established, and accepted, it would be possible to protect these great animals, and entrust the future research and scientific work to the nation.

10 Whatever can it be?

The simple answer to this question—assuming that one considers it worth the asking—is that no one knows what the Monster is or, more correctly, of what species it may be.

Most investigators, and I was certainly one, start with some good ideas about identity, but as they progress they become less certain. Ultimately they come to appreciate the level of their own ignorance—but from this commanding position it is possible to gain a wider view of the probabilities.

Anyone who seriously examines the evidence at Loch Ness, and at Morar and Shiel which are still very close to the sea, must recognize the fact that since the last Ice Age these lochs were connected with it.

A further examination of reports from the sea itself, and from the western Scottish seaboard in particular, will indicate that similiar 'phenomena' have been reported, quite reliably, both from long ago and from the very recent past. This lends credence to the view that the large unidentified aquatic animals in these lochs, as reported, are the descendants of previously marine animals which were cut off from the sea centuries ago, and have adapted to a freshwater environment. The only possible alternative is that they still migrate to and from the sea through subterranean links.

It seems probable that these animals are descendants of a previously known species, which may have evolved considerably; but it is just possible they may prove to be a previously unknown *type* of animal. No one but the zoologists and biologists can speak with authority on an issue such as this, although everyone has the right to an opinion, and is certainly free to express it.

At present there are five main theories as to what the Monster could be. They all have merit, and each has found support at one time or another. They have one thing in common. None of them entirely fits the evidence, and each has serious technical shortcomings. These theories are:

1. that the Monster is a mammal, a huge unknown type of long-necked seal, or Giant Pinniped.

2. that it is a huge unknown form of amphibian, a sort of monstrous newt, with a long thin neck.

3. that it is an evolved form of long-necked Plesiosaur, a parentally marine, saurian reptile supposedly extinct since the Cretaceous period 70 million years ago.

4. that it is an invertebrate—perhaps a type of huge aquatic worm, or other boneless creature.

5. that it is indeed a fish—a colossal adult eel, the 3-ft larvae of which has already been found in the sea.

There is one other theory to which the great majority of people subscribe, even today; and that is the 'good for hotel business' theory; which of course is obviously valid. The Monster is good for business, and will certainly remain so, even if the theory fails to explain away the other tiresome evidence.

Commander R. T. Gould, in the early 1930s, examined various animal types as possible contenders for the title, and found them wanting: Aquatic birds, salmon, otter, porpoise, tortoise, turtle, catfish, eel, ribbonfish, bluga (or any other known species of whale), sturgeon, crocodile, known seals (walrus, sea-lion, sea-leopard and sea-elephant), shark, sunfish, ray, and giant squid. There is no reason to doubt the conclusions of this brilliant man. Nor is there any reason to accept the alternatives put forward frequently by members of the 'lunatic fringe', of whom there are many at the loch.

The fact remains that until we film the Monster clearly, in good definition, or secure a small piece of tissue from him, or even catch a specimen, the fascinating problem posed by his identity remains, and is open to discussion.

Unquestionably the most interesting discussions develop between people who are prepared to admit they could be wrong. In weighing up the pros and cons of these theories, it is interesting to note that the 'mammal' theory has some weighty technical opinion in support of it today, as the 'amphibian' theory had some years ago. The 'giant eel' theory which first came into fashion was the first to go out of fashion—only to re-emerge quite recently. The 'reptilian' theory (and Plesiosaurs in particular) has for long been in the balance, with some good points in its favour, and some bad ones against it. People like Gould, who first subscribed to it, tended to veer away upon consideration. The 'invertebrate' theory has had its brighter moments, but has had some telling points made for it—particularly by F. W. Holiday, in his recent book *The Great Orm of Loch Ness*.

At the present stage of investigation, one can only guess what the Monster may turn out to be—the important thing is to proceed, and find out.

Personally I am committed to obtaining results which will make the Monster's existence accepted as a fact. Its identification, I consider a matter for experts in zoology. Having seen the beast, I know it is an unknown animal, so it should prove of interest to them.

From a practical viewpoint there is one aspect of the Monster's behaviour which has always intrigued me—its ability to sink straight downwards, as evidenced once more at close range in the 1963 fishermen's account (see p. 121). To do this the animal must be able to alter its displacement at will.

Ivan T. Sanderson, F.L.S., F.R.G.S., F.Z.S., a zoologist of wide experience, published a table of characteristics for types of aquatic animal, as a foreword to my first book published in the United States, in 1962. He used the headings 'inflatable air-sacs (external)'; 'inflatable air-sacs (internal)'; and 'hydrostatic organs (other)'. Amphibians score 'YES, YES, YES', reptiles 'NO, NO, NO', and mammals 'YES, YES, YES'—which is disappointing for the Plesiosaur people!

During my researches for *The Leviathans*, I came across a most unexpected source of reference. As an engineer I found it intriguing, and as a monster-hunter I thought it a possible missing piece in the jig-saw puzzle. I was reading *Geology and Minerology*, by Professor William Buckland, F.R.S., published in 1837. In chapter 14, 'Proofs of Design in the Structure of Fossil Vertebrate Animals', Buckland analyses various extinct animal forms, among them the Plesiosaurus *P. dolichodeirus*. The first specimen was found in England, about 1823, in the lias of Lyme Regis.

The ribs are composed of two parts, one vertebral and one ventral; the ventral portions of one side uniting with those on the opposite side by an intermediate transverse bone, so that each pair of ribs encircled the body with a complete belt, made up of five parts . . . from the form and capabilities of these fossil ribs, we infer that they were connected with vast and unusual powers of expansion and contraction of the lungs. . . . The compound character of ribs probably also gave the Plesiosaurus the same power of compressing air with its lungs, and in that state taking it to the bottom, which we have considered as resulting from the structure of the sterno-costal apparatus of the Ichthyosauri.

The fact these observations were made a long time ago does not necessarily invalidate them. Buckland was a brilliant man. He established the first readership in geology at Oxford, and was largely responsible for the 'natural sciences' being included among the subjects in which undergraduates might be examined for a degree, in 1850. It should be remembered too that perhaps the greatest paleontologist of all time, Baron Georges Cuvier, died as long ago as 1832.

Looking at the skeleton of a long-necked Plesiosaur today, this curious rib-structure is clearly in evidence. One can appreciate how it would function mechanically giving the animal the power to alter its displacement at will, and thus rise or sink vertically.

But this does not mean that Loch Ness is populated with Plesiosaurs, any more than with giant eels, or colossal amphibians, or seals, or invertebrates. It is not for me, an aero-engineer, to pontificate. It should be remembered too that Gould subsequently favoured the amphibian theory, which has some nice things about it. Elizabeth Montgomery-Campbell, founder member of the Loch Morar Survey team, has in her possession sketches made by a witness: he reported seeing at Morar a 'monster lizard' some 20 ft long, lying on the bottom in 16 ft of crystal water, on 8 July 1969. The bottom at this place is white sand, and small leaves were visible on it. Only the front part of the animal was seen clearly, including a snake-like head, wide mouth and slit eyes. Two pairs of limbs were in evidence, the front pair having three digits. I have seen these sketches, and the impression they give is of a newt-like animal, but it should be remembered the witness was fishing in a small boat and that . . . 'the shock of seeing it caused him to rev. up and get away as fast as possible, so that he only saw it momentarily.' (Account no. 14 of the Historical Section, *Report of the Loch Morar Survey* 1970, 24 November 1970.)

Finally it is an encouragement to note that during the last decade there has been a change in the attitude of many people towards the Loch Ness research—although at the present time it is still voluntary, self-energizing and dependent on subscription, and the earnings from its own hard work. More and more individuals, and groups, and scientific people are lending their support and equipment in an attempt to help solve the mystery, which genuinely remains one of the greatest unsolved mysteries on earth.

The human story represented is as entertaining, and extraordinary, as the Monster is itself. In a third and last book, *Project Water Horse*, I hope to record something of it: the fears and excitements, the humour and success of a drama set against the backdrop of two majestic Highland lochs, and played out across the surface.

I am not yet certain of the ending, but in the course of a decade I have watched the plot develop, and an almost empty stage slowly fill with characters—each with a part to play, a contribution to make, however small—to the whole tremendous story.

Appendix

In order to bring this third edition of the book up to date it is best to list events chronologically and as simply as possible. Only in so doing can the multitude of happenings be put into perspective.

1972

Loch Ness—last year of LNI's fieldwork based at Achnahannet which was subsequently closed down. No conclusive photography obtained, but a short 35 mm. sequence of movie film was shot through a long lens off Fort Augustus, showing twin 'plumes' of displaced water in Borlum Bay.

Academy of Applied Science team headed by Dr Rines scored a decisive underwater success in Urquhart Bay, assisted by LNI crew aboard *Narwhal*, in use as a station boat, monitoring a Raytheon sonar chart machine. A second workboat, with Carol and Bob Rines aboard operated the Edgerton strobe-set. In the early hours of 8 August large intruding echoes appeared on the sonar, and the flashing strobe-set recorded photography of parts of a large moving object, or objects within the sonar beam.

Last year of fieldwork for Loch Morar Survey team, following publication of *The Search for Morag* by Elizabeth Montgomery Campbell and Dr David Solomon—which summarised the work already done in 1970 and 1971 with 33 sightings recorded, and a biological assessment that 'the level of productivity of the loch is capable of supporting a population of large animals.'

TD's programme: six weeks' lecture tour in the USA for the Academy of Applied Science—talks given at MIT, Eastman Kodak, the Boston Aquarium, various universities and at Scripps Oceanographic Institute in southern California. Private discussions held by RHR and TD at the Jet Propulsion Laboratories in Pasadena—the world's leading authority on the new technique of computer-enhancement of photographs. Visit paid to Disney Studios to view comically animated semi-documentary 'Man, Monsters and Mysteries' filmed by producer Ken Peterson at Loch Ness in 1969.

Expeditions: eight weeks' boatwork in *Hunter* on Loch Ness, two weeks on Loch Morar helping LMS team. Results: new witness tapes and a 'disturbance' sighting on Morar from the deck of *Hunter*.

Publications: series of three articles for *Photography* magazine, and first paperback edition of *Loch Ness Monster*.

TV and radio: in USA interviews arranged by British Tourist Authority went out on network TV and radio through some 550 stations; in UK though BBC's 'Late Night Extra', 'Start the Week', 'Springboard'; Southern Independent TV's 'Day By Day'. Film making included some work with Japan's NTV and a documentary made with NAVPROS TV about the work aboard *Hunter*—and the 'Monster Mystery' as seen through the eyes of a child (star performance by the youngest Dinsdale, 12-year-old Angus, born on the night of the *Panorama* programme in June 1960)—which was to become an award-winning film in Japan.

1973

Loch Ness—The LNIB assisted a Japanese expedition which promised much, and achieved little due to its failure to import a submarine and other items of equipment. This expedition attracted world-wide publicity, and some ribald comment too. Dan Greenburg writing for America's *Oui* magazine published 'A Penetrating Account of a Big Game Hunt that Never Quite got Beneath the Surface', immortalised by sub-heading quotes: 'If your Royal Highness wish me to kill monstuh, I kill monstuh. I give head to Queen Elizabeth, give one frippa to Princess Anne, another frippa to Mao Tse-Tung, another. . . .' Mr Toshio Kou, the expedition promoter, gained the admiration, if not the love, of Monsterhunters for his quite unique performance—and for 1973 the unchallenged title 'The Year of the Japanese'.

Academy of Applied Science team under RHR aided by Ivor Newby in *Kelpie* and TD in *Hunter* and numerous other British hands tried out a new sonar trigger linked movie-camera station underwater—monitored from Basil Cary's yacht *Smuggler*, as station boat in Urquhart Bay. This experiment ran for three months and several triggerings resulted, but due to the ice-water environment the lubricant 'gummed up' and the bank of four cameras failed to operate. Diving operations for set-up and recovery were completed by Ivor Newby, and Lee Frank a competent American student. Station recovery in September was filmed by the BBC's 'Blue Peter' team, and put out on TV later.

TD's programme: photographic drifts in *Hunter*, ten weeks on Loch Ness. Two weeks ashore for tripod work. Tapes of new sightings recorded, including an 'out of water' account from a

Mrs Margaret Cameron, a life-time resident of Fort Augustus, and a school-boy group sighting of a big animal seen at very close range—initially only ten yards away. Copies of this tape were made and sent to the Scottish Economic Planning Dept (via the Office of the Secretary of State for Scotland) and the Scottish Nature Conservancy Board.

Publications: Lead article in the April edition of the *Photographic Journal* of the Royal Photographic Society describing briefly the August 1972 Academy sonar linked underwater strobeflash photography—with full-plate photograph of the large flipper-like appendage recorded some 45 ft underwater, coincident with massive sonar intrusion of a moving object 20–30 ft long 'as determined from the length of the echo' having a sudden 'echo protruberance' with a dimension of about 10 ft. 600 copies distributed to museums, zoological societies, universities and schools in Britain, with 400 copies dispatched to the Academy in Boston, for similar treatment.

The Story of the Loch Ness Monster, published in paperback (at 25p) for young people, by Target Books, and by Allan Wingate in hard covers.

Lectures, TV and radio: Two weeks' lecture tour in USA— Exeter and Boston, New York, Washington DC, Orlando and Miami. Ten UK lectures. One short documentary made with NTV of Japan at Ness and Morar, and one at Ness with BBC Scotland's 'Macleod at Large' TV series. Interviews with BBC's 'Blue Peter' and Radio 4's 'Kaleidoscope', in London.

1974

Loch Ness: LNIB ceased organised field operations, and discontinued membership due to rising overhead costs—but remained in being as a 'research organisation'.

NIS (*Ness Information Service*) bi-monthly newsletter commenced circulation in January, prepared by Rip Hepple, a former Group-commander and resident staff member of the LNI expeditions of 1970 and 1971—subscribers invited to apply directly to him at Huntshieldford Cottage, St Johns Chapel, Bishop Auckland, Co. Durham, DL13 1RQ. (Sub: £1·25 in the UK and $7.00 in the USA and Canada.)

Academy of Applied Science team under Dr Rines imported highly sophisticated automatic trigger-sonar station. Efforts to set this up underwater in Urquhart Bay with help of Caledonian

Canal crew aboard barge *Lochalsh* ended in disaster. One professional diver quitted out of fear, while on the job, and the station tipped over on the bottom, damaging equipment. Later, in July, experimental runs in TD's *Water Horse* with Raytheon deep-mapping sonar produced unique evidence of shape of rock-walls of Great Glen cleft, beneath the bottom silt. Returning from the USA in September, checks were carried out from *Malaran*, a 12 ton research vessel up from the Clyde, which established that the sonar pulse is indeed penetrating the silt some 1,800 ft beneath the bottom.

TD's programme: Hunter with 50 h.p. Mercury outboard and Mk 9 Jaguar tow-vehicle withdrawn from service, due to rising fuel costs. *Water Horse* recommissioned with 20 h.p. Mercury and A 40 as tow-vehicle. Loch Ness expeditions Nos. 26 and 27 mounted in her June–July, and No. 28 aboard *Malaran* in September. Journey from Firth of Clyde by sea via Loch Fyne, Crinan Canal, Firth of Lorne and Caledonian Canal to Fort Augustus took five days due to 'storm force 10' gales *en route*. In December assistance was given to Peter Self of Canon Records Ltd to help obtain voice tracks of Monster witnesses for a new LP about the Highlands: 'Come to Scotland—a souvenir in pictures, words and music', containing a poster showing some of the most important Monster photographs.

Loch Morar pilot expedition and trials of submersible observation chamber *Machan* designed, built and tested by Mr Adrian Shine, and assisted in the field by students of the Royal Holloway College. Results satisfactory. Equipment functioned safely at 20–30 ft, and was proof tested to 60 ft.

New books published in 1974: *In Search of Lake Monsters* by Peter Costello (Garstone Press, London) and *The Loch Ness Story* by Nicholas Witchell (Terence Dalton, Lavenham, Suffolk); both in hard covers. The latter book was received with enthusiasm as a comprehensive historical record, important for collectors.

1975

Loch Ness: Academy of Applied Science team under Dr Rines imported miniature computerised sonar-trigger underwater station, and purchased *Hunter* with 50 h.p. Mercury, to act as workboat— also a new inflatable Avon dinghy named the *Noo-scow* (successor to TD's ageing *Moo-scow*). Work was started in Urquhart Bay in June, with bottom station rigged some 80 ft down, and the flashing Edgerton strobe-set trailed overnight from the stern of *Hunter*, swinging free and down about 30 ft. Within eight days two sonar intrusions triggered twenty-three photographs, and cassettes were recovered from the strobe-set. Test runs were made with mapping sonar and Loran C navigator set which proved immensely accurate. Recovery of underwater station is effected with the aid of pro. divers Jim Buchanan the scientist director of Undersea Vision (Scotland) Ltd and North Sea diver Andy Wheeler, aiding the experimental team of Rines (electronics) Needleman (logistics) and Dinsdale (operations).

Results from this work produced several dramatic colour photos from the strobe-set, but the sonar-trigger station pictures appeared to be blotted out by (possibly) a silt cloud, stirred up from the bottom. Analysis of these results, and further information gleaned from the computer study of the 1972 series of underwater strobe-set pictures, prepared the way for a scientific symposium, and a press conference to be held at Edinburgh in December of 1975.

Loch Morar: six weeks of fieldwork put in by students from the Royal Holloway College, with Adrian Shine as leader. Base camp established on one of the islands—and almost the entire perimeter of Loch Morar scanned to a depth of 30 ft, using *Pequod*, a specially designed fibreglass boat, with a perspex dome in the bow, offering a fish-eye view of the bottom. No bony remains were found, and due to the failure to gain permission for *Machan* to be used from the shallow sandy bay at Meoble, its potential was limited. The *Pequod* was holed on a rock and the crew had to swim for it; and with the flooding of an underwater video-scanner and torrents of rain and gales to contend with at the surface, the expedition was somewhat 'up against it'—but retired in good order, proving that misfortune is no bar to enthusiasm. The search programme in *Pequod* covered nearly 200 miles of water in five weeks, in proof of this.

TD's programme: Loch Ness expeditions Nos. 30 and 31 in May-June and July yielded more sighting tapes, a personal Nessie V-wake sighting (not filmed), a visit from Peter Byrne and Celia Kileen from the Big Foot Information Centre and search HQ near Dalles, Oregon (visited by Rines and Dinsdale in 1972)—and brief trip to Morar with them—interviews with Finnish radio and a Swedish convention in Pitlochry.

Between these two expeditions *Water Horse* was storm driven on the rocks and holed, but saved by Fort Augustus Abbey schoolboys moments before sinking—then patched up with fibre-glass. In June, time was spent re-fitting *Hunter* before launching to move up-loch to Academy mooring in Urquhart Bay. Expedition No. 32 in August-September included visits to Morar to work with the Royal Holloway College/Shine expedition, and produced tapes of new giant back sightings in both lochs, and wake sightings with speeds reported of up to 25 knots. Expedition No. 33 in October assists RHR with more overnight strobe-set operations in Urquhart Bay, which are not productive and records a 'near miss' back surfacing at Fort Augustus, which was spotted by a witness at half-mile range some 4 degrees outside of tripod mounted camera scan.

Lectures, TV and radio: Flight to Brussels in March to address 'Les Reserves Naturelles et Ornithologiques de Belgique' followed by a three week tour in USA to speak at six Kentucky universities (host, Prof. Henry Bauer), an all-black high school in Miami, and on two network TV shows and six radio shows in New York. Academy conference in Boston. In UK: talks given at Royal Holloway, Radley, and Cheltenham Colleges. Interviews with Scottish TV's 'Scotland Today', Capitol Radio's 'Hullabaloo', LBC's 'Nite Line', BBC's 'World at One', 'Good Morning Scotland' and 'Postmark Africa', Sveriges Radio AB, Stockholm, Oxford Radio, and NAVPROS TV from Japan.

Publications: *Project Water Horse* in June (Routledge & Kegan Paul in paperback and hard covers)—being the author's personal account of the human aspects of the chase, its humour, and the more bizarre experiments.

The ill-starred 'Edinburgh Symposium' and what happened afterwards

Due to the extraordinary complexity of events, and the rate at which they occurred unexpectedly, it is necessary to end 'Loch Ness 1975' with a separate explanatory note which puts them into perspective.

Shortly before departure for the June series of experiments at Loch Ness, Bob Rines was invited to Slimbridge, home of the exotically beautiful 'Wildfowl Trust' where Sir Peter Scott lived. Sir Peter had been active in the early 1960s at Loch Ness, after coming to my home to view the 1960 film. Subsequently he became a founder member of the LNIB, and was largely responsible for the Linnaean Society meeting in London in 1961 at which the case for the Monster was put before a panel of senior zoologists—without any noticeable effect. In the years that followed his name remained on the LNIB letterhead but he took no active part in the decade of LNIB field expeditions as his time was occupied with work for the World Wildlife Fund and the Survival Service Commission of the International Union for Conservation of Nature, of which he had become chairman. His sudden reawakening of interest in the Loch Ness phenomenon was occasioned by the 1972 'flipper' picture, the significance of which was obvious to him; and this was heightened by the new underwater photography obtained in June, by our Academy experiments, and also by the new long range still photography shot on 18 July by Mr Alan Wilkins at Invermoriston Bay. Alan was a classics master at Annan Academy, and when on holiday at Loch Ness with his wife and two children early one morning he had been witness to a display of large-hump surfacings, and movement which showed them to be animate. His sequence of still photographs shot through a 640 mm. Novoflex lens at a range of some 3,500 yards produced measurable images, but the 16 mm. movie film shot through a Bolex 16 mm./300 mm. lens was less successful.

These results were the subject of a hastily convened LNIB directors' meeting in London, and were subsequently reported in the *Field* in two splendid articles, one 'Life in the deep in Loch Ness' by David James on 23 October—which reviewed the subject as a whole, and 'Monster: the four vital sightings' by Alan Wilkins on 27 November. Both were entirely clear, and objective.

Coincident with all these happenings and news of the underwater strobe-set pictures obtained in June, Sir Peter Scott's unequivocal statements on radio that in his view the 'flipper' picture shape was distinctly like that of the plesiosaurs lent support to the visual comparison made between the photo and a diagram showing the limbs of long necked plesiosaurs, in my April 1973 article for the *Photographic Journal* of the Royal Photographic Society. Furthermore, he painted an artist's impression of two 'Nessies', each with a double pair of such limbs and put this on exhibition in London, with other of his incomparable wild-fowl paintings . . . the stage was set.

Precisely what was to happen on that stage time was to demonstrate but, in keeping with the general atmosphere of progress and excitement, plans were laid for a presentation to be made through the Coelacanth Committee of the Royal Society in

London, but due to lead-time problems and other considerations these were modified to appear as invitations to the 'Sir Peter Scott Symposium' to be held in Edinburgh on 9 and 10 December, under the auspices of the Royal Society of Edinburgh, with joint sponsorship of the University of Edinburgh and Heriot-Watt University.

The release of these 'confidential' invitations to principals of the monsterhunting fraternity, senior members of the scientific community, politicians, local dignitaries from Loch Ness and others who held a particularly important view or position inevitably caused a 'leak', which added something to the cascade of 'leaks' which had already occurred on both sides of the Atlantic, and through the printing of a small paperback for Penguin—*Loch Ness Story* by Nicholas Witchell, a law student who had put in much time at the Ness. It contained dramatic descriptions of the new underwater pictures, but was not due for publication until 11 December, and there was a strict embargo on it. Sadly, the press failed to honour this and the flood-gates of unwanted publicity were opened wide which—with a whirlwind betting spree occasioned by Ladbrokes the bookmakers offering (initially) odds of 100: 1 against the Monster being verified by the British Museum within one year of the bet being made—caused an immense balloon of rumour, fiction and utter nonsense to inflate.

But like all artificial bubbles it could not sustain itself, and burst with a thunderous percussion, and the news that the 'Edinburgh Symposium' had been cancelled—as indeed it had! On 1 December 1975 the Royal Society of Edinburgh issued a letter entitled:

Edinburgh Scientific Symposium on evidence for and against a 'Loch Ness Monster'
. . . When a Symposium to present new and review past evidence for the existence of unidentified animals in Loch Ness was first proposed by Sir Peter Scott, as Chancellor of the University of Birmingham, its local organisation was accepted by the Royal Society of Edinburgh acting in association with Edinburgh and Heriot-Watt Universities. The programme was to be that on the first day evidence should be submitted by invited experts to a restricted scientific audience and that an agreed press release would be made the following day.

It was understood that by this means, a forum would be offered for the free expression of opinions and criticisms so that a balanced assessment of the evidence could be prepared for the public.

Recent wide publicity, from prospective participants on both sides of the Atlantic, at variance with this understanding has forced the Royal Society of Edinburgh and the Associated Universities to the regretful conclusion that no useful or impartial discussion can take place at this time, and under these circumstances.

Accordingly, the Royal Society of Edinburgh, the University of Edinburgh and the Heriot-Watt University are no longer prepared to be associated with the meetings arranged for 9 and 10 December.

This somewhat haughty pronunciation was to cause an international shockwave of surprise, and a vacuum of anticlimax. The Monsterhunters were stunned, and not a little disgusted. So much voluntary effort had been put in by them, as usual at their own expense—but, as events were to prove, it was not the end of the matter.

David James, the unquenchable Executive Director of the Loch Ness Investigation Bureau through all its years of sweated effort had always maintained a 'press on' initiative, and as a Member of Parliament had already booked a Committee Room at the House of Commons, the Palace of Westminster, for a meeting to follow the Edinburgh affair, at which the main participants, MPs and members of the House of Lords who showed an interest would be welcomed; and he decided not to cancel it.

This meeting took place in the ancient and historic Grand Committee Room, after two days of preparation and fervent co-operative effort between the LNIB principals, the Academy team, scientists and independents such as myself who had all contributed something to the years of search and research effort. Opinion indicated that the time had come to fight, and that the best place had been chosen.

Shortly before 8 o'clock drinks and light refreshments were served at the St Stephen's Club, at which last minute adjustments were made to the planned two-hour presentation. Acquaintance-ships were renewed and the magic of human personality allowed to mix and blend together with a drop of two of the elixir, known to Highlanders as the 'water of life'.

'Running order' for the presentation was listed as follows: 'Lord Craigton (in chair), 3 minutes—Norman Collins, ditto—

David James, 5 minutes—Sir Peter Scott, $7\frac{1}{2}$ minutes—Dr Robert Rines, Dr Edgerton, Mr Klein, Mr Wyckoff, Mr Olaf-Willums, Mr Blonder, together 40 minutes—Sir Peter Scott (to introduce zoologists), 5 minutes—Dr Zug, Dr McGowan, Prof. Roy Mackal, 30 minutes—Sir Peter Scott to read extracts from the British Museum, etc.—David James introduces [witnesses with supporting photographic evidence]—Tim Dinsdale/film, 10 minutes—R. H. Lowrie, 5 minutes—Alan Wilkins, 5 minutes—David James speaks on conservation and introduces Richard Fitter, 5 minutes—Sir Peter Scott opens meeting for questions, 35–40 minutes—Lord Craigton closes meeting, with final words by Norman Collins.'

In the event, the presentation overran to some extent, leaving perhaps 20–25 minutes for questions from the floor—the press, the British Museum and other senior scientists. Members from the Commons and the House of Lords numbered perhaps a hundred, and there were many famous personalities who had at one stage or another taken part in the operations, TV and radio discussions. It was a lively meeting with powerful deliveries made for both sides of the argument—feelings were aroused and spear-like verbal thrusts delivered.

There was no obvious victory for the Monster protagonists, despite the power of the technology and the facts it represented, nor was the British Museum's stand of 'not proven' acceptable to all.

The result, on the face of it, was a draw, but this did not stop the many discerning folk within the 'body of the kirk' from drawing their own conclusion based on what they had seen and heard in the presentation—but as far as the outside world was concerned, still bemused and reeling from the plethora of nonsense-press they had been subjected to, little or nothing had occurred, for the simple reason that the House of Commons meeting was virtually ignored by the media.

The reason for this was not immediately obvious, but there were probably three contributory factors. First, the general public was 'full up to here' with the Monster, the underwater photographs, 'Dr Rines and his Academy', etc. Second, a press-conference called the afternoon before the meeting, by Sir Peter Scott and Bob Rines disclosed the Monster's new Latin name *Nessiteras Rhombopteryx*, to be published next day with an explanatory article in the scientific journal *Nature*—along with the 1972 sonar chart, the 'flipper' photos and the startling 1975 picture we had obtained in June some 35 ft underwater, showing what appeared to be Nessie's head, long neck, and part of its great body. This meeting, in the opinion of many, distracted attention from the evening's undertakings, which were in any event late—if not actually past the 'going to bed' time for newspapers. This third factor combined with the stone-wall tactics put up by senior members of the British Museum staff convinced the press that the show was already over, and apparently not worth reporting in detail. It was a pity, because the House of Commons meeting was the most important event ever to be recorded in the Monster's long and torturous history of attempts to get the facts put forward openly and regarded seriously. In comparison with some of the rubbish that had gone before, its high technology message and equally its marvellous significance virtually went by default. However, the *Observer* on Sunday 14 December did publish a piece by Pearson Phillips—'Nessiteras absurdum', which must rank as a fair example of modern journalism in which the iceberg tip of facts emerge from beneath an overlay of innuendo, and blasé criticism based on the shifting sands of 'instant-expertise'—but it made good entertainment and to some extent was edifying. It is as well for us at times 'to see ourselves as others see us'—but the risk with any form of entertainment writing is that wit predominates at the expense of accuracy: and of a balanced commentary. For example, (from para. 2) . . .

It was when Dr John Sheals of the Natural History Museum rose from a cluster of his colleagues and, quivering with professional indignation shot the whole presentation to pieces with one carefully prepared broadside. There was, he said, no evidence to show that any of the photographs taken by Dr Robert Rines and his Academy of Applied Sciences team were of the same object let alone of a living animal. As for Sir Peter Scott's article in the scientific magazine *Nature* (awarding the beast the formal scientific name of *Nessiteras rhomboteryx*), that was spreading a 'false notion of reality' and adding disgracefully to the 'clutter of dubious names'. . . .

This takes no account of the statements published at the presentation, from equally eminent scientists, which accept the photographs as real, and showing parts of animals. Furthermore, within the *Nature* article there are two successive photographs, taken about a minute apart, which are obviously of the *same* flipper-like object attached to the same body behind it.

In respect of the above, it is as well to note what these scientists actually did say about the photographs:

Dr G. R. Zug, Curator, Division of Reptiles and Amphibians, Smithsonian Institution (a personal view): 'The 1975 film includes several frames containing images of objects which possess symmetrical profiles which indicate that they are animate objects or parts thereof. I would suggest that one of the images is a portion of a body and neck and another a head. . . . I believe these data indicate the presence of large animals in Loch Ness, but are insufficient to identify them?

Dr C. McGowan, Associate Curator, Dept of Vertebrate Palaeontology, Royal Ontario Museum, Canada (a personal view): 'I have no reason to doubt the integrity of the investigators of the Boston Academy of Applied Science, nor the authenticity of their data. . . . I am satisfied that there is sufficient weight of evidence to support that there is an unexplained phenomenon of considerable interest in Loch Ness; the evidence suggests the presence of large aquatic animals. . . .'

A. W. Crompton, Professor of Biology, Harvard University, Director, Museum of Comparative Zoology: 'I personally find them extremely intriguing and sufficiently suggestive of a large aquatic animal to both urge and recommend that in future, more intensive investigations similar to the type that you have pioneered in the past be undertaken in the loch.'

From these three statements alone (there are several others) and disregarding all the technical evidence put forward, interpreting sonar charts, and previous surface photos, and my own film, it is clear that Dr John Sheals' comments did not shoot 'the whole presentation to pieces', as so glibly stated by Mr Pearson Phillips, in whose article no one escapes ridicule for he later refers to Dr Sheals and his four senior zoologists as 'The Kensington Five', and zoologists as 'touchy people at the best of times' who 'when they see amateurs inventing new animals after a few summers spent dipping cameras into the water get upset'.

This latter comment may be true in the sense that none of the Academy team were trained zoologists, but in the field of technology and operations, which gained the results, we were hardly 'amateurs'. Dr Harold Edgerton who prepared the camera strobe-set *advises* Cousteau on his underwater techniques, is an Honorary Fellow of the Royal Photographic Society and a Professor at MIT; Bob Rines is a physicist who trained under him, a famous patent attorney, an electronics expert and inventor; and I, as an ex-aeronautical engineer, have 21 hard-earned letters and have been a technical representative for firms like De Havilland and Rolls Royce. Our divers were both men of particular accomplishment, and Jim Buchanan has since been invited to join the Academy and has been awarded a Fellowship at Stirling University where he studies virus infections in shell-fish through an electron microscope! These facts hardly come through in the *Observer* article—but it is of little consequence.

Time alone will establish precisely what is and what is not true under water at Loch Ness. Time and the continuing efforts of a wonderful, stimulating band of dedicated men and women— who are the true explorers; and who enjoy a sense of humour which carries them through the good times and the bad.

The day that the Latin name *Nessiteras Rhombopteryx* was published, anagram specialists pointed out that when juggled about the letters could read 'Monster Hoax by Sir Peter S' which dismayed the Monsterhunters; but Bob Rines soon came up with the antidote, another anagram—'Yes, both pix are Monsters. R.'